PENDULUM CRAFT

PENDULUM CRAFT

YOUR GUIDE TO USING, CHOOSING & UNDERSTANDING PENDULUMS

FOX TAYLOR

AUTHOR OF *SIGIL CRAFT*

STERLING ETHOS
New York

STERLING ETHOS
New York

ISBN 978-1-4549-5570-2
ISBN 978-1-4549-5571-9 (e-book)

Library of Congress Control Number: 2024944504

For information about custom editions, special sales, and premium purchases, please contact specialsales@unionsquareandco.com.

Printed in China

2 4 6 8 10 9 7 5 3 1

unionsquareandco.com

Cover and interior design by Carlos Esparza
Cover art by Fox Taylor

**To the raccoons
who live near my house.
I have no proof, but I think
you'd love pendulums.**

CONTENTS

INTRODUCTION

"We begin to suspect that the stuff of the world is mind-stuff."

—ARTHUR EDDINGTON, ***The Nature of the Physical World***

I started working with pendulums around the same time I started really exploring witchcraft and magic as a whole. Something about these crystal and metal teardrops suspended from delicate chains seemed alluring and mysterious to me. I started to develop a small collection of pendulums, but I didn't really know anything about them or why someone would use them. And while I've always been fascinated by ideomotor responses, which has manifested in a fair collection of Ouija boards, I hadn't taken the time to dive more deeply into how they worked or what they were all about. Sure, I was the kid who would pull out wooden letter game pieces and one of my dad's Robbie Burns whiskey glasses to use as a makeshift planchette, arranging the letter pieces in a circle on the table, often terrifying and fascinating my friends. But even then, despite people telling me that the "messages" I was receiving were really just muscles in my hand acting of their own accord, combined with my own subconscious, I just felt like there was something more to it. But what?

I am a rational person who makes decisions based on peer-reviewed articles, logic, and reason. But I also choose to leave room for the possibility that there is more to life than how we collectively define physical reality. My North Node in Capricorn and my various Capricorn rulings and placements see to it that I am very driven to seek out information and truth, but I am also a very watery being, with major placements in water signs driven by dreaming and intuition. I like answers, but if they have witchy or magical underpinnings . . . I'm not going to turn away from that or ignore it. That's why I take everything with a level of mystical optimism, because I'd rather believe in the What Ifs and the Why Nots of the world. Life is too short to only believe in what others say.

In this way, I was drawn to pendulums, not just because of the science behind them, but because of the mystery, because of the wonder and curiosity. Pendulums, once I started wanting to understand them more intimately, presented this mysterious thing that I could never quite crack. Being tasked with writing this book presented me with the opportunity to explore this arcane implement at length. Because while I have worked with pendulums, made and collected pendulums, and written pendulum zines, prior to researching this book, I never fully understood them on either a scientific or an esoteric level. As Richard Webster writes in his introductory guide *Pendulum Magic for Beginners*, "Pendulums are deceptively simple"—I would have to agree. Still, I think their simplicity is misunderstood. For such rudimentary tools, they hold an incredible expanse of knowledge, history, and possibility.

There have been so many attempts made to imbue the history of pendulums with an excess of exoticism and mysticism by misappropriating and oversimplifying. In this book, I aim to demystify the pendulum and how we understand it. The histories of the pendulum and its sibling divination practices are as diverse as the possibilities of the pendulum itself.

The writing of this book has been an interesting process. While I researched, I also experimented with the pendulum in ways that I never thought I would. It's been a surprising process, but at times a frustrating one. The frustration could be seen as a bad thing, but I do think that frustration is a feeling that should be a part of the magical journey. Frustration is born out of a drive to do something, a desire to pursue something that is somehow important to you. We become frustrated over things we care about. At least, that's how I feel, born from my own personal brand of neurodivergence. When I care about something, and there's some kind of obstacle, or it's more difficult than I expected, I get frustrated—not because it's difficult, but because I want to be able to do it without difficulty. There will be times in life where you want to pursue something, but for whatever reason, you hit a blockage or meet a limitation. It's not always a reason or an invitation to give up. It's more of a reason to re-evaluate and try to understand something in a way that works for you. Sometimes frustration is born because we're trying to work the way someone else says to, instead of figuring something out for ourselves or working in a way that works for us. That's why this book introduces a variety of ways to work with pendulums, in hopes that you will find a method that works for you and feels comfortable and good. Pendulums are not one-trick ponies. They're powerful multiuse tools, with numerous possibilities for anyone who wishes to give them a try. In this book, I also offer ways to channel a pendulum's capabilities without using an actual pendulum. I want to keep options open for my disabled friends and comrades who might have trouble with hand dexterity (pendulum chains really aren't designed for all people).

As always, I aim to be as inclusive as possible, but I will be the first to acknowledge that I am only human. If something in this book doesn't resonate, I encourage you to take what does and leave the rest. Nothing is one-size-fits-all, and magical theory is no different. Witchcraft, divination, anything spiritual or magical—it's all meant to be developed and learned by the individual. While some (including myself) can offer tools, suggestions, and guidance, it is paramount that you feel comfortable in what you're practicing. That feeling of comfort is from your gut and your intuition, the most powerful divining tools of them all. Trust those tools, and let everything else offer support along the way.

A note on sources of information: This book was heavily researched, and I went down a lot of rabbit holes to find prudent information. However, it is my due diligence to mention that some of the information I share in this book was channeled—that is, pulled intuitively from the aether and put to paper. Interestingly, this is how a lot of spiritual information is gathered, and has been gathered in the past. If you see something written here that seems to conflict with something you've read elsewhere, I invite you to not see it as a conflict, but rather a new perspective, and an addition to the lexicon of magical knowledge. I also invite you to create your own correspondences (the symbols and physical items or materials that relate to a particular intention, deity, planet, etc.) by communing with plants, minerals, animals, and spirits. You may unlock divine information that is completely unknown, but a deep truth nonetheless. You never know what you might stumble upon by just listening to the world around you.

THE HANGED MAN AS PENDULUM

In the past year, The Hanged Man has made itself known in my everyday life through symbols and images. I wrote a short piece on Instagram deconstructing the concept of The Hanged Man/The Hanged One/Suspension. That short essay made me deeply uncomfortable with the card. In the following months, The Hanged Man was a constant presence in my day-to-day life, as if asking me to reconsider the card, get familiar with it, and even return to its more metaphysical meanings.

I am bringing up The Hanged Man because there are a lot of similarities between this tarot card and the thesis that exists around the pendulum, as presented in this book. The Hanged Man is practically the ruling card for this book, and the experience I had writing it. The Hanged Man is a visual proxy for the pendulum as a divinatory tool.

Let's look at The Hanged Man for a moment. Rachel Pollack, a science fiction and comic book writer who wrote extensively on the tarot, gave The Hanged Man the keywords "attachment," "suspension," and "unconventionality." She described the upright card meaning as "Attachment to deep values. Seeing things differently than those around you. Joy, even revelation. Alternatively, being stuck, or a sacrifice."

The Smith-Waite deck describes the card as "Wisdom, trials, circumspection, discernment, sacrifice, intuition, divination, prophecy."

Eden Gray, American actress and tarot writer, describes the card as "surrender to a higher Being causes a reversal in one's way of life. In spiritual

XII
THE HANGED MAN.

matters, wisdom, prophetic power, self-sacrifice. May also mean suspended decisions, a pause in one's life." She also states that "the figure suggests a reversal of the mind rather than of the body." In *Mastering the Tarot,* Gray offers the interpretation of "spiritual growth, surrender to a higher wisdom. A complete reversal of one's usual way of life. Dependence no longer on the self but on the Creative Intelligence that runs the universe. Material temptations should be conquered. A period of indecision in one's life. The ability to prophesy to some degree."

A suspended body. Decisions. Differing perspectives, unconventionality. Spirituality, and the Creative Intelligence of the universe and the aether.

For a long time, I interpreted this card as one of self-sacrifice and altruism, but the card is far more about spirituality, self-discovery, and changing perspectives. This will be obvious to many, but sometimes the true meaning or essence of something is blocked from us until we're ready. This is part of the spiritual journey: not getting something until you do. It is a journey of growth. To think you understand everything from the get-go is limiting to your personal growth and opportunity for exploration.

The Hanged Man is a pendulum. A suspended body, inviting us to look at things from a different angle, and be open to possibility. Like The Hanged Man, the pendulum encourages us to get specific, but keep ourselves open to something different, and maintain an open mind. We are asked to respect and understand that we might not get the answers we want. We are asked to be open to different ideas, to different opportunities in the realm of the spiritual and divine. The Hanged Man, and the pendulum, remind us that nothing is permanent or fixed, but rather that everything, ourselves included, is always in a state of flux and movement. As science fiction author

Octavia E. Butler says in her novel *Parable of the Sower*, "The only lasting truth is change."

We are invited to look at the minute movements and details, to be open to shifts and differences that may make themselves known. Nothing is permanent, and there are lessons in that.

Every state in which the pendulum exists is temporary, and every time it moves, it is following the same trajectory, but each time it is changed, the pendulum experiences this routine in new ways. The repetition is a pattern, but each movement is new. The pendulum is us. The pendulum is the human experience.

Part 1

WHAT IS A PENDULUM?

Chapter 1

THE HISTORY OF PENDULUMS

It could be argued that pendulums have always existed, and like physics in general, it's just that we didn't have language for them. But this is an oversimplification, especially in terms of human achievement. It's incredible to recognize these early uses of math and science among the ancestors of the world, especially when we notice that we still use some of the tools today.

The earliest written record of someone using something like a pendulum to divine information is from Ammianus Marcellinus, a Roman soldier and historian from the fourth century CE. In book twenty-nine of *The Roman History of Ammianus Marcellinus,* he references an individual performing a ritual in which he placed a round dish inscribed with the letters of the alphabet upon a tripod ("in the likeness of that of Delphi"), over which "he balanced a ring which he held suspended by a flaxen thread of extreme fineness." The ring "touched and bounded" off the different letters on the dish, and from these letters the diviner spoke verses that corresponded to the questions that were being asked.

Divination was a fairly common practice in ancient Rome, but the use of a pendulum as divination isn't common. It is more common to see examples of haruspicy (divining information by examining the entrails of an animal), or augury (interpreting the movement and behavior of birds). Most divination was done to determine the will of the gods.

Meanwhile, we have the plumb bob, a tool used in construction, carpentry, and surveying. It is a simple weight (usually with a pointed end) suspended from a line. A plumb bob is used to determine if something is vertically straight, by working with gravity. Plumb bobs existed in ancient Rome, ancient Egypt, ancient Peru, and in other times and places around the globe. When observing a plumb bob, purely from a metaphysical perspective, they look exactly like pendulums, and it's more likely than not—in the infinite expanse of time, space, and human history—that someone in ancient times used a plumb bob for divination. That's cool to think about, but as a logic-driven individual with a love for math and science, I think the practical uses are at least as interesting. There is a distinct possibility that the ancients did use plumb bobs to divine information, but it's not up to us to speculate or rewrite history in a way that benefits us.

PENDULUMS THROUGHOUT HISTORY

In scientific fields, "pendulum" refers to a device that is made of a weight suspended from a pivot, allowing free movement. There are dozens of types of pendulums, both theoretical and real. Many are mathematical models, or examples of physics in action. Pendulums have been used for timekeeping (the first pendulum clock was invented by Christiaan Huygens in 1656 and was the standard model for timekeeping until the 1930s) and measuring (including accelerometers and seismometers).

The story goes that Galileo Galilei started studying the properties of pendulums after observing the swinging of chandeliers in a church. A 1602 letter is the earliest surviving document of Galileo writing about pendulums, and his hypothesis of isochronism in pendulums (theory pertaining to the repetition and uniformity of a pendulum's motion, and the fact that its movement happens at regular intervals).

One of the most famous examples of a pendulum is Foucault's pendulum, invented by Jean Bernard Leon Foucault in 1851. Foucault lacked formal training in science, but still theorized that he could use a pendulum to show the rotation and movement of the Earth. The pendulum would appear to move, but in reality remained stationary while tracking the Earth's movement. It was the first successful demonstration of the Earth's rotation that did not depend on celestial observation. In February 1851, Foucault sent a notice to the scientists of Paris, which read: "You are invited to see the world turn." The first demonstration of Foucault's pendulum was indeed a success, as has been every demonstration around the world ever since.

At one point, magic and science were united through the art of alchemy. Alchemy combined what we understood about science and the natural world, with what we felt or believed about the unseen and metaphysical worlds. Nowadays, magic and science are often separated into two distinct worlds, but I don't think this is necessary. Such a harsh divide can (and has) led to things like the "crunchy to alt-right pipeline," in which people who are interested in natural forms of living and alternative spirituality are directed toward white supremacist and alt-right dogma, often by way of social media algorithms and online community overlap. Wanting to live more "naturally" (whatever that may mean) does not mean being free from science. But everything—including all of science—comes from nature. There is no part of us that is separate from nature, no matter how much we try.

Pendulums are an example of magic and science coexisting. What is a magical tool is also an example of physics at work, and vice versa. I don't know what all of these long-dead scientists would think if they could see that we're using pendulums to communicate with spirits, our higher selves, and the beyond. Maybe they would see it as a waste, or maybe they would be fascinated. Maybe the integration of pendulums into the magical world would have inspired them. We can never know for sure. But I choose to embrace the juxtaposition of magic and science that is a pendulum. Science is magical. Magic can be scientific. The two are not mutually exclusive, nor will they ever be.

PENDULUMS, DOWSING, AND DIVINATION

The history of pendulums is closely connected to the history of dowsing and divination. The ways that people in antiquity used divining rods is often conflated with pendulums. We don't know exactly who first used the pendulum for divination, but magical divining rods seem to be a part of human history. At its core, a rod, a staff, whatever it is, is magical. The fact that a tool like a cane can help someone walk is already magical. A staff was a precursor to a cane, and it conjures the image of a divine individual or wizard. Staffs have big sorcerer energy, and we should see canes in the same magical light: a magic wand offering support, relief, control. That is divine.

Dowsing and Radiesthesia

Dowsing is believed to date back thousands of years. Some writers see Moses drawing water from the stone as being an example of dowsing, but I would consider that to be more of a mystery, a miracle, made of something divine. Dowsing is the act of using a tool (usually a forked stick, but other tools can be used) to find something. The goal is usually to find underground water or veins of metal within the Earth, but dowsing can also be used to find lost items, specific materials, or even people.

A cave painting at Tassili Najjer in the Sahara, which dates to approximately 6000 BCE, has a section depicting an individual carrying a forked stick in their two hands. It does look like someone using a dowsing rod. Of course, we can't say with absolute certainty that this painting illustrates the act of dowsing, but sometimes the simplest explanation is the correct one. If this is true, then we are continuing to use and practice techniques that are over eight thousand years old.

Perhaps that's why we want so desperately for pendulum reading to be something ancient, done by humans who lived millennia before us. It creates a feeling that we are connected to the past in a specific and tangible way. To know that we share something with the ancient world is alluring, validating, and even comforting.

Radiesthesia (the perception of waves) is the physical ability to detect radiation emitted from a person, animal, object, or place. J. Cecil Maby, a prolific dowser and radiesthesist, defined radiesthesia as "the faculty and study of certain reflexive physical responses of living tissues to various radiations . . . resulting in displacement currents and other inductive effects in living tissues." Maby distinguished radiesthesia from psychic abilities and the practice of divination, though in the writings of other radiesthesists the line isn't quite so clear. Radiesthesia is used broadly in a variety of ways, but it all comes back to an ability to discern the vibrations and radiations coming off of the body—living, organic, or inorganic.

The term "radiesthesia" was coined by Abbé Alexis-Timothée Bouly, a French dowser. The earliest written use of this word may be in an article from the October 30, 1926, issue of *Le Journal*, a Parisian newspaper that wrote about Abbé Bouly. This is also the source of one of the only photos of Bouly.

Abbé Alexis-Timothée Bouly

Dowsing has been around for a very long time. People have looked at ancient records like art (including cave paintings) and writing, and insist that this is proof of ancient dowsing, but it's all conjecture and speculation. There is a distinct possibility that dowsing has been performed for thousands of years, but I'm reluctant to take the writing and artwork available as irrefutable proof.

Dowsing is typically done with Y-rods (twigs or sticks in the shape of a Y) or L-rods (metal rods that swing over each other to form a cross), but dowsers have used a number of tools for centuries. In the 1876 book *Curious Myths of the Middle Ages,* S. Baring-Gould includes a chapter on the divining rod, discussing early references to what could be described as dowsing. Some of the historical records referenced could be misinterpretations, but there is a reference to a fifteenth-century Benedictine monk named Basil Valentine, who wrote about workers in mines using rods to find metals. Valentine included a list of the names by which these rods were known, and this combination of information points to pretty solid proof of dowsing being used at this time. Dowsing is most commonly used for water and metals, but there are references to people using dowsing to find stolen items, dead bodies, and criminals. Once people started writing about dowsing in greater detail and with more specificity, there are examples of people writing about clever uses for dowsing, many of which continue to be used by dowsers today.

Radiesthesia is a direct relative of dowsing, though its exact inception is unknown at worst, and vague at best. The rise of radiesthesia does seem to correlate to the rise in popularity of pendulums among dowsers, though use in dowsing does predate the coining of the term "radiesthesia," at least based on photographs from 1913 of the Dowsers Congress, which shows a group of men holding dowsing rods and pendulums. The more popular radiesthesia becomes, the more references to pendulums we see.

Radiesthesia started to gain more popularity in the 1930s, when the overlap between the occult and the metaphysical became more pronounced.

Dowsing Congress showing off their pendulums, 1913

Most writing from this time comes from France, where star players, including dowsers and radiesthesists like Andre de Belizal, Leon Chaumery, and Antoine Bovis, expanded upon their ideas. These three men get referenced a fair amount in terms of pendulums, credited with the discovery of ancient "pendulums," as well as the invention of other tools that align more specifically with radiesthesist practices and theories that they coined or conceptualized, including Pyramid Power and the Atlantis Ring. I won't go into either topic too deeply, because 1) it is not completely relevant to the topic at hand, and 2) it is a rabbit hole that gets too weird for me as an individual and a writer. I won't discount anyone's beliefs without trying my best to understand them first, but the idea of someone dying and being found mummified because of too much Negative Green is too much for me.

When it comes to using pendulums, there is a considerable overlap between divination, dowsing, and radiesthesia. The operator is given similar instructions for all three, but in terms of discussion, there is generally a lot of distinction between them, in spite of all three being considered quackery, pseudoscience, or complete "woo-woo" among skeptics.

What Is Divination?

While we're on the topic—what is divination? In its simplest terms, divination is the practice of accessing information by means of specific tools or a system of interpretation. Historically, divination has been used to forecast the weather, determine the gender of a baby before birth, find out who one's future spouse would be, as well as accessing virtually any information someone might want, for political, spiritual, or personal reasons. If someone had a question, there would likely be a way to divine the information. Many forms of divination are named to have the suffix "-mancy," which means "divination by means of." Ergo, if you see a word ending in "mancy," you can safely assume that it is referring to a divinatory practice.

Divination styles and tools are as varied as people and cultures, varying in complexity and popularity. Some people may find themselves well suited to one type of divination, while others may feel it is challenging or impossible. The key is to find what resonates with you as the practitioner. At the end of the day, all divination is a way to access information by means of an intuition trigger or spark.

Pendulum divination is only one of thousands of schools of divination. In the realm of pendulum dowsing and divination, there are a few other styles of divination that get conflated, which I have included here. They're similar in some ways, but largely unrelated. Still, in the spirit of dispelling myths and inaccuracies, let's look at a handful of examples.

Cleidomancy

In recent years, cleidomancy has been distilled down to mean any form of divination with a key, especially if the key is being used as a pendulum. Honestly, it's an understandable evolution. "Cleido" comes from the ancient Greek κλείς or *kleís*, meaning key or collarbone. So, technically any divination with keys would literally be cleidomancy, but historically, cleidomancy is more specific and specialized.

Cleidomancy, in its most traditional sense, utilizes a Bible (or any book), a string, and a key. Arthur E. Waite (of Smith-Waite tarot fame) writes in detail about cleidomancy in his book *The Occult Sciences.* By Waite's count, there are three methods traditionally used to determine the name of a suspected individual, or to find lost things. Like any form of divination, you can use cleidomancy to answer any questions, and by its nature, cleidomancy works best with yes/no questions. The easiest way to practice cleidomancy is to take a book (it doesn't have to be a Bible) and close a key inside it (about halfway through) with the handle of the key poking out of the side. The book is then tied shut very tightly with string. You want to be able to lift up the whole book by the key and have the key shift very little, if at all. The book can be kept like this, as a permanent divinatory tool. To ask the book questions, you hold the key between your two index fingers. When you ask a question, the book will remain stationary for "no" and will turn for "yes."

Coscinomancy

This one often gets confused with cleidomancy. Coscinomancy is a form of divination that uses a sieve and a pair of shears. The shears are opened wide and the blades are wedged into the edge of the sieve. This combination is held upright by two individuals, each supporting it with one finger. The diviners ask a question, and the sieve rotates if the answer is "yes," or remains stationary to indicate "no." Like cleidomancy, this technique is primarily used to determine the name of someone who committed a crime or misdeed.

Rhabdomancy

"Rhabdomancy" is a term that is used to describe any divination practice that uses sticks, wands, or rods. Older methods of rhabdomancy involved setting a staff or rod on its end and interpreting how or where it fell. Nowadays, it is used primarily in reference to dowsing techniques that use a forked stick or metal rods.

All divinatory practices have their merit. They're just not meant to be confused with pendulum divination on a whole. Pendulum divination (which we could, perhaps, call pendumancy?) is the practice of divining information using a pendulum.

Chapter 2

DISPELLING MYTHS AND UNTRUTHS

While researching this book, I found myself surprised by all of the myths and untruths I saw perpetuated in countless articles and books. It's amusing to imagine certain things to be true, but misinformation is still misinformation. Before we go further in this book, I wish to address some myths about pendulums and dispel some pervasive illusions. Let's give history the respect it deserves, and play from fact, rather than trying desperately to make things fit. Trust me, it doesn't make anything less interesting or magical.

Some things in the ancient world certainly look like modern pendulums. And, as I've mentioned, there's a lot of overlap between dowsing and pendulums. I read so many articles and narratives pointing to ancient Egypt and saying, "Look! Pendulums!" On the surface, this seems like a simple way to trace this instrument's lineage. But alas! History requires context, and some digging. Let's look into some of the ways that the history of pendulums and pendulum divination is commonly explained, and review the proven facts that can help us evaluate the reality of the situation and cut through the misinformation.

MERKHET

Called an "instrument of knowing" by the ancient Egyptians, the merkhet is a tool that was used for surveying and timekeeping. The design is, at its most basic, a plumb bob (also known as a plumb line or plummet) attached to a wooden handle. A plumb bob is a weight (often with a pointed tip) suspended from a string. This tool is used as a vertical reference in carpentry and masonry. Plumb bobs have been used since ancient times across several cultures, used to ensure that constructions are "plumb" or vertical. A plumb bob can also be used in surveying, usually in conjunction with other instruments.

Early scientific tools are so often interpreted to be magical instruments, which is wild to me. Isn't their status as scientific advancements at least as interesting and magical? The merkhet has met that fate, with many writers pointing to it as a ritual object meant for metaphysical purposes. However, the merkhet was, by all accounts, used only for surveying and timekeeping, as well as tracking the alignment of certain stars called decans or baktiu. When visible, these stars would be used to keep track of time at night. This was convenient, because otherwise the only form of timekeeping known was the sundial, which, of course, couldn't be used after the Sun had set. And the merkhet was a crucial example of the nascent art of keeping time: one of the few remaining artifacts dates back to 600 BCE.

At a glance, merkhets do look like another divinatory tool called the itombwa, a rubbing or friction oracle. The itombwa was created and used by the Kuba people in Central Africa. Made up of two parts, the larger piece is carved in the shape of an animal, with a smaller piece meant to be rubbed on the back of the animal carving.

WADJ AMULETS, EGYPTOLOGY, AND CULTURAL MISAPPROPRIATION

The reason there is a pervasive theory that ancient Egyptians used pendulums for divination exists for reasons beyond the fact that Egyptians would use plumb bobs for carpentry and masonry. The main reason is

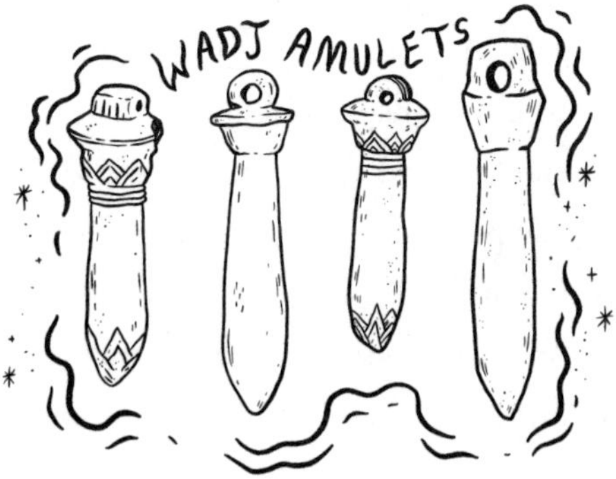

linked to the early-twentieth-century fascination with Egyptology among European dowsers and occultists. From the late nineteenth century up until about the 1940s, there was a lot of attention on Egyptology. Several styles of pendulums that make appearances in occult spaces are based off of the so-called pendulums found during this time.

Egyptology has been a favorite topic of many occultists, who would point to examples from ancient Egypt as evidence not only for their beliefs and to validate their ideas, but also to inspire. Some shapes of pendulums have their origins in Egyptology, found during the practice of what can only be described as grave robbing. There are a lot of questions around the ethics of early archeology, with its influences and effects still being felt today. It is all a direct result of white entitlement and colonization. Most archeology has resulted in the theft of artifacts and spiritual items, to which the colonizer does not have any real claim. Even taking historical and spiritual items out of context in the ways people do is a direct result of colonization, as we see in the case of these mysterious pendulums. After all, using someone else's history and artifacts to fill in gaps in one's narrative is a pretty glaring example of a colonizer mindset. The act of taking without permission is typically frowned upon, but even now, appropriation and misappropriation get a lot of passes.

Antoine Bovis was an iron monger and hardware store owner. He was also a radiesthesist. His "claim to fame" is Pyramid Power, a pseudoscience theory that the pyramid as a shape holds great power, including the ability to mummify and prevent food from rotting. He developed this theory while on holiday in Egypt in the 1930s, and at this time he discovered wadj amulets in tombs. He insisted they were pendulums. He wasn't the only one to connect these dots. Andre de Belizal and Leon Chaumery both created pendulums using the wadj amulets as inspirations, though less information exists about these men. Chaumery and de Belizal found that the shape of the wadj amulet emitted a type of energy that makes it suitable for communication. Perhaps, given the wadj amulet's relationship to the afterlife, this is true.

Wadj amulets do look like pendulums. They are usually a long tapered shape, with a hole for a string at the top. One could look at a wadj amulet (also known as papyrus scepters or papyrus columns) and see how it could be used as a pendulum. One could, in theory, use one of these amulets as a pendulum.

So what is a wadj amulet, really? A wadj amulet is in the shape of a papyrus stem, made of turquoise feldspar or Egyptian faience. Faience is a material considered magical by the ancient Egyptians, made from common materials like quartz, alkaline salts, lime, and mineral-based colorants. This material was highly regarded, along with precious stones and metals. These amulets appear to have been the most popular during the 26th dynasty (circa 664 to 525 BCE), although the Coffin Texts from the Middle Kingdom (2055 to 1650 BCE) reference wadj amulets.

Wadj means "green" or "fresh," and these amulets evoked life, vitality, and regenerative power, which were qualities desirable for both the living and the dead—the hope being that these qualities would allow the dead to have a good afterlife. The importance of these amulets is expounded upon in the *Book of the Dead.* Spells 159 and 160 discuss the charms, including the material from which they were made, as well as where they should be placed on the deceased. When individuals have written about these amulets, erroneously describing them as pendulums, they note that they have been found in sarcophagi, but it is never really called into question. But why would people be buried with pendulums?

A wadj amulet is a protective talisman worn by the deceased. They are ever-present in the tombs of ancient Egyptians, who believed that if a wadj remained intact, the deceased was doing well in the afterlife. But the fact of the matter is that wadj amulets were funerary in nature—nothing points to their having been used for divination, let alone as pendulums.

I am concerned about the notion of these amulets, and any funerary amulets, being removed from the tombs of the dead, and I am concerned about individuals using them for divination. Surely ignoring things like curse tablets and tampering with the ancient Egyptian dead has had some negative repercussions. In my experience, every ancient Egyptian exhibit at a museum is haunted, carrying an energy of fear, anger, frustration, and several other emotions that I can't really put into words. I do believe in curses, and that includes the Egyptian curses placed by priests with the intention of protecting the dead. Are there ancient spirits that connect themselves to wadj amulets, and maybe even the pendulums that are shaped like them?

What if there are ancient Egyptian entities that see these pendulums shaped like wadj amulets, and don't know how to react, or what to do with the information? I'm not saying that any ancient cultures or individuals have ownership over certain shapes, but what kind of consequences are waiting for us when we tamper with the idols of afterlives that are not our own?

I'm reluctant to recommend any of the pendulum shapes based off of ancient Egyptian amulets, because the energy is fraught with difficult layers of taking what does not belong to someone, as well as the perpetuation of colonizer mindsets. Maybe there are some things better left alone. I address and describe the shapes later on, but I avoid these shapes. I'm sure that there is some validity to the other pendulums created by these men (Bovis, Chaumery, and de Belizal), but for the sake of decolonization, for the sake of radical witchcraft and divination, I think there are better results to be found experimenting with other ideas (and creating new ones). For the sake of education and reference, all of these will be discussed later, but it is important to remember that just because something is taught or presented for educational purposes, doesn't mean that you must embody or use it. Sometimes information is presented for the sake of "here's what *not* to do."

ZHANG HENG SEISMOSCOPE

Zhang Heng was a first-century polymath living in China during that Han dynasty who created the first seismoscope (a simplified seismometer, an instrument used to indicate the occurrence of an earthquake). Zhang's seismoscope no longer exists, but some have tried to recreate it using writing and descriptions from the fifth century CE.

Zhang called his seismoscope the Houfeng Didong Yi, or "instrument for measuring the seasonal winds and movement of the earth." The instrument was like an earthquake weathervane in the form of an intricate metal urn. It is theorized that the device worked by using an internal pendulum that would push a marble-like ball into a toad-shaped container, not only indicating the direction of the earthquake, but also acting as a kind of alarm system. However, no one is exactly sure how the seismoscope worked. At the time of Zhang's innovation in first-century China, no one knew what caused earthquakes, or even what they really were. Beliefs were primarily informed by the book *Yijing* (*Book of Changes*), which suggested that earthquakes were caused by cosmic disturbances based on yin and yang (yin and yang being the dual forces in the universe that oppose each other, and through that opposition create balance). Some also thought that they were caused by the heavens' displeasure with current rulers, and the poor treatment of common people.

During the Han dynasty, many scientists, including Zhang Heng, believed in the *Feng-chiao* (the oracle of the winds, a form of divination that interpreted the direction, force, and timing of the winds to determine what was going on in the cosmos and thus predict events on Earth). I'm including this here because during my research, I came across writing that mentioned an ancient Chinese practice of using pendulums to drive away wind demons. I couldn't find anything to back this up. I can't say with absolute certainty, but my theory is that misinterpretations and misunderstandings around Zhang's seismoscope, and the prevalent use of divination, may have contributed to the idea that pendulums drive away wind demons. We will never really know Zhang Heng's intentions or how his mechanism worked, but it is a marvel of early mechanical engineering.

THE MYSTERIOUS EMPEROR KWANG SUNG

In the many books and articles about pendulums that I read while researching this book, especially within the context of dowsing, writers mentioned Kwang Sung, an ancient Chinese emperor, who is often shown holding what could be described as a dowsing fork. I decided to dig into this. Surely, if so many people mentioned this individual as an early dowser, the information would be easy to find.

I'm not sure who first wrote about this so-called Emperor Kwang Sung, but as far as I can see, such a person never existed. The legendary (used here in the literal "may be a legend" sense) figure depicted in the image that people point to is Kuang Yu, known as Yu the Great. The image in question is from the west wall of the Wu Liang Shrine, in which several legendary rulers are depicted. Yu is credited with the first successful state efforts to control floods, featuring prominently in the Chinese legend of "Great Yu

Controls the Waters." The tool Yu is shown holding may be an agricultural tool, a status symbol, or something to do with flooding, based on other artwork from similar time periods.

When people talk about this mythological Kwang Sung, they are referring to Yu the Great, who would have existed during the Xia dynasty, but the dates proposed for his reign predate the oldest known written records in China. Yu may not have existed, but he plays a vital part in Chinese folklore and legend. I can understand how someone could take the idea of Yu implementing flood control, and interpreting it as Yu controlling the waters, which would make the fork-shaped tool look even more like a dowsing rod, given the relationship between dowsing forks and finding water. It is a tremendous leap in logic, but I can see how someone might form these connections, especially when they are already trying to make pieces fit a theory.

HISTORICAL MYTH, POPULAR NARRATIVE, AND THE OCCULT

In 1983, Marion Zimmer Bradley published *The Mists of Avalon,* which explores Arthurian legends through the perspectives of female characters. My first introduction to the concept of this book was during a group meditation as part of a virtual witchcraft retreat. The individual leading the meditation seemed to be taking us to a real place, but my spouse explained to me that Avalon is a mythical place. Later, after the retreat, they explained that Bradley is an alleged child abuser and rapist, with convincing evidence against her. How can someone claim to be a feminist when her life is built upon the abuse of children, including her own? Bradley did not conceptualize Avalon, nor did she create the women in these stories. Many critics re-reading *The Mists*

Culturally Sensitive Information

In this world, we will encounter information that is closed to us. We are not meant to know everything or have access to it. While researching this book, I found a reference to plummets currently in the Smithsonian Institution Archives (a plummet being another term for a plumb bob, but usually referring to something that might not be the specific shape of a plumb bob). However, there are no photographs of these objects, and limited information. The extent of the information offered is that the plummets came from the Eastern Band of Cherokee Indians. There are no photographs because the plummets hold spiritual significance, and knowledge about their use is therefore closed to anyone who is not part of the Cherokee Nation.

Finding this was one of the more humbling aspects of my research for this book. It was an important reminder that although information exists, it is not always ours to partake in. I am choosing to mention this because, in an age of information, it is always tempting to dig deeper, to uncover secrets. None of us are owed answers or explanations, and sometimes it is our responsibility to accept that and move on. When white people take and abuse so much of this world, we are not owed more. We can accept what we have and be respectful enough to not push boundaries.

Am I curious? Of course. But the information around these plummets is not mine to have, and it's likely not yours, either. The lesson is to not dig when all signs say "No digging here."

of Avalon now suggest that the book is actually women-hating and anti-feminist. Even before Moira Greyland (Bradley's daughter) came forward about her abuser, some critics were already questioning whether *The Mists of Avalon* was actually feminist literature. Still, interest in the spiritual aspects of Avalon created a small movement of people who began to reconsider Celtic spirituality and religion. The book conjured ideas of Anglo-Saxon and Celtic paganism, inspired by the mythology of Arthurian legend, finally with a perspective that is more female- and goddess-based.

By the time I heard about Avalon, transported there through a guided meditation, Bradley was already accused of sexual abuse. It's impossible for an individual to be aware of everything happening in the world, and all newsworthy events, but it still put an uncomfortable veil over the meditation and that experience. I do believe that it's possible to separate the art from the artist, but what happens when an individual's work is completely interwoven with someone's understanding of their own spirituality, and that becomes perpetuated? If you pull the thread on any individual's life, you're likely to find something that would make them worthy of being cancelled, and each of us must decide on our own where we draw the line of personal comfort and morality.

Fiction can, and does, influence our lives.

Fiction can, and does, influence our human experience. Fiction readily influences spirituality. When I started reading Octavia E. Butler (a thankfully noncontroversial and nonproblematic figure), I found that her Earthseed writing resonated with me on a deep level. Earthseed is a fictional religion within the novels *Parable of the Sower* and *Parable of the Talents*. The scripture that Butler created spoke to me and my own spirituality, allowing me to redefine and reconsider some aspects of my craft and how I view spirituality and my relationship with higher powers.

"All that you touch
You Change.
All that you Change
Changes you.
The only lasting truth
is Change.
God
is change."

—OCTAVIA E. BUTLER, *Parable of the Sower*

This quote has stuck with me, permeating my everyday life, my art, myself. Who am I to judge if people find similar spirituality through books like *The Mists of Avalon*?

I think the biggest difference is the acknowledgment of origin. I know that Earthseed was created by a mortal woman. A woman so mortal that she never completed the Earthseed trilogy. I can recognize that this divine truth I feel in my bones was created by an individual, who lived, learned, created, wrote, imagined, and eventually experienced a human death.

Narratives like *The Mists of Avalon* run the risk of being too close to the actual mythology, blurring the line between ancient paganism and modern human perspective. I was made to believe that Avalon was a real place, and that everything surrounding it was a reflection of ancient belief, channeled by a modern individual, who was charged with the responsibility of bringing these ancient secrets to us. In reality, it is just more modern imagination. A fabrication.

Channeling has its place in books and information, but when it starts to blur the lines of real history, it can be a huge problem. Integrating false or misleading narratives, regardless of origin, is how misinformation happens, sometimes leading to harmful and damaging ideas.

I'm bringing all of this up because of Umberto Eco's 1986 book, *Foucault's Pendulum.* What happens when someone reads something and doesn't know that it's fiction? Can fictional ideas be twisted and manipulated until they are believed to be historical fact? When someone does an internet search for pendulums, they will likely encounter something to do with Umberto Eco's book, but that is because the search engines we use can only search based on the information and keywords that we give them. Can this little bit of confusion lead to someone thinking that Umberto Eco's book is all fact, and not a work of historical fiction? I would like to give readers more credit, but then when I'm fact-checking claims that the Knights Templar created or used the Hebrew pendulum, and the only results for "pendulum+templar" or "pendulum+knights templar" or "knights templar pendulum" is Umberto Eco's *Foucault's Pendulum,* I start to get a little concerned. The fact that the Foucault's pendulum is a real thing can further blur the lines for someone who might not be thinking too deeply, or just not paying attention. A lot of us don't anticipate a need for critical thinking when we're just doing a basic internet search.

In the realm of pendulums, Umberto Eco isn't the only one who may have created a mythologized version of history in people's minds. In 1842, Edgar Allan Poe published his short story "The Pit and the Pendulum," about an individual being tortured during the Spanish Inquisition. The story horrified readers. The story went on to be adapted into several films and TV episodes, and this started to cement the idea of this torture as something that happened during the Spanish Inquisition. In reality, the torturers during the Spanish Inquisition could not spill blood. This rule meant that there was a lot of license for creativity, but it also means that an instrument like a pendulum that cuts the individual would not have been an acceptable option. This torture was described by Poe, and it's possible that Poe got the idea from the one book that describes this torture, *The History of the Inquisition of Spain* by Juan Antonio Llorente, published in 1826. This record is based on secondhand information, which Llorente likely misunderstood. The closest thing to a pendulum-inspired torture device was the strappado, in which the arms and legs of the accused were tied behind their back, and then a pulley system was used to lift them up, suspending them from the ceiling.

Works of fiction can lead us to create our own lore, mythology, and ideas. Fiction can carry truths, but it's not wise to look for historical fact in works of fiction. Foucault's pendulum is a real object, but just as the locations in a book may be real places, it can be expected that the author will take artistic liberties in order to tell the best version of their story. These imagined realities do not indicate any truth or fact. Search engines don't (and can't) distinguish fact from fiction. The two can interweave, both intentionally and unintentionally. Humans are fallible, and we are imaginative creatures.

I don't know for certain that Umberto Eco's book led to the idea that the Knights Templar are involved in the history of pendulums, but I think it would be too much of a coincidence to imagine anything else. Eco is not responsible for this kind of misinformation. He was writing fiction. Bradley isn't responsible for individuals believing that Avalon is real, and Poe isn't responsible for people thinking that there was truth in his work. We as the consumers of media are responsible for how we interpret and understand the works. We can refer to others' understandings, and those perspectives can shape our own. Unfortunately for some, fiction and nonfiction alike don't usually come with a user's warning.

I don't hold the creators of work responsible for misunderstandings of their work, but everyone can hold themselves accountable if their work is leading to too much confusion. I do hold people accountable and responsible when they misquote and perpetuate myths and falsehoods. In the case of the occult, witchcraft, and metaphysical, too many people will hold themselves in positions of having all of the answers and all of the information, and then will use their space and apparent authority to mislead. Maybe it's not intentional, but doing things like perpetuating an idea that the Templars were somehow involved with the history of dowsing and radiesthesia is irresponsible, to say the least. Working in spaces and using ideas that are unprovable by science (i.e., magic) does not excuse us from living in the real world, or having an awareness of how actions can benefit or harm others.

The magical and the occult worlds have countless unreliable narrators. An unreliable narrator is, in literature, a narrator who misleads the audience or reader, either deliberately or unintentionally. The unreliable narrator often excludes information, either because they are withholding it completely, or they don't have the information themselves, as a character. I'm introducing this point because so many so-called authorities within magical and divinatory spaces are unreliable narrators, pretending to have all of the information, but in reality, they are lacking key points. Instead of admitting the lack of information or understanding, they will often fill in the gaps. Occultism and magic should be collaborative spaces, and individuals contributing new ideas and concepts are generally welcome. However, instead of providing anything new in an honest way, these unreliable narrators will attempt to pull from history, from other cultures, twisting and appropriating ideas to fit their personal narratives, while also indicating that the idea is not at all new, but ancient and esoteric. We trick ourselves, and others, into thinking that something being old makes it more true, and more reliable, when in reality we as a civilization are always evolving and developing for a reason. We are not meant to live in the past, and we are not meant to misunderstand the past for our own gains.

We are told to believe the past, but we are actually meant to learn from it. Sometimes that includes being skeptical of the past and how things were done. The past is interesting and relevant, don't get me wrong. But just like fictional stories, it can't be our only frame of reference.

None of this is to say that we can't get useful information from these unreliable narrators. But just as they exist in the literary and storytelling worlds, perhaps we should see these occult and magical narrators as a means to move the plot forward, rather than being our only source of information. We don't owe them anything, but we do owe it to ourselves and the future to be somewhat skeptical and critical when someone gives us information. We should always question things, especially if it doesn't seem totally right. An honest person will understand if you don't believe them and want to double-check (present author included), but the people who try to prevent you from asking questions do not have your best interests in mind. The people who withhold information or try to prevent you from digging deeper only have themselves in mind. These people know that they don't benefit from you having the information. But you will.

Chapter 3

PENDULUMS, SPIRIT BOARDS, AND BEYOND

"The result of a research is due neither to the divining rods or the pendulum, they are simply visual indicators of muscular reflexes, it is due to my active desire to find the answer. It is my instinct or unconscious that may answer in the form of nervous or muscular reaction, of which I am unaware, causing this instrument to move."

—ANTOINE LUZZ, ***La Radiesthesie Moderne,*** **1943**

Pendulums seem so very magical. There's something so fascinating about the pendulum swing, as it always seems to swing by itself, almost by magic. Which might raise the question . . . is there someone controlling it? Is there some kind of spirit pushing the pendulum? In short: yes. In a manner of speaking. It's you. You are the spirit making it move.

There are many different thoughts and opinions on this, depending on what you are trying to do with said pendulum. In terms of divination, let's say you are doing a pendulum reading, trying to get information on something spiritual or what-have-you. You ask a question, and the pendulum starts to move, likely indicating yes, no, unsure . . . The pendulum is being moved by you.

Skeptics often dismiss pendulums as useful tools because of the ideomotor phenomenon, also known as the ideomotor response or reflex, in which an individual makes motions unconsciously. It usually occurs outside of the awareness of the individual. Our bodies are always moving, whether we are actively aware of these movements or not. Our muscles twitch and our organs go about their work of digesting, breathing, and so on without our full awareness. The reality is that our brains are constantly sending messages to every inch of our bodies, whether we know it or not. These micromovements and automatic muscular reactions can result in things like moving a planchette on a spirit board or causing a pendulum to swing—we may not know we're doing it, but our bodies are making decisions all the time without our conscious input.

Let's say that our bodies are purely responsible for these forms of divination. Does that really mean that we need to dismiss the messages that come through? If one is using a pendulum and the messages they are receiving are resonant, that's really all that matters. There is always the risk that any form of divination or psychic messaging might not be helpful. There is always the risk that the reader is fraudulent, or simply doesn't know what they're doing. Still, that's not always going to be the case, and if you are receiving helpful information that resonates deeply, the goal of the divination is ultimately accomplished. It doesn't really matter how that process looks, as long as it is working.

Our bodies are powerful diviners, with or without other aids. We talk about "gut feelings" for a reason. Bodies ache when the weather is changing. Breasts let someone know when it's time to breastfeed their child. Anxiety can cause an individual to have involuntary movements. Our bodies can tell us when we need a specific nutrient. Our physical forms communicate needs through discomfort or pain, and are always telling us things. Sometimes our bodies pass along messages from the subconscious, playing off of instinct and intuition. If we listen to those messages, why not listen to those communicated by our bodies when they cause a pendulum to swing? Why dismiss a divination tool because it might be our bodies causing the movement?

There have been a number of board games and toys created that used pendulums, including Kreskin's ESP. These could actually be used as a pendulum, but they were sold as novelty (and varieties of novelty pendulums are still sold today). Meanwhile, there are other games and tools that may use the ideomotor response but could still be used as divinatory tools, including those discussed in the following sections.

TALKING BOARDS

Talking boards, also known as spirit boards or witch boards, are the wood or cardboard boards with letters, numbers, and some words like "yes" and "no." "Spirit board" is a broad term for all of these items, which include Ouija boards. ("Ouija" is actually a licensed name, currently owned by Hasbro, which is why I won't be using this terminology.) The first talking boards are estimated to have been created and used in the late 1880s, and the Ouija board was patented in 1890 by Elijah Bond.

The talking board is used by placing fingers on a piece of wood or plastic called a planchette (usually a kind of heart shape with a hole in the middle, but other shapes exist). The planchette then moves around the board, answering questions by pointing to letters and numbers. Talking boards are widely considered evil, but they are sold in toy stores, so like anything, their morality is very much dependent on the intention with which they're used. It's important to remember that *anything* can be haunted, anything can be cursed, and anything can be used to summon unsavory entities.

A talking board can be used by itself to communicate with spirits or the subconscious, but can also be paired with a pendulum instead of a planchette, in which case the pendulum would indicate which letters are needed to spell out the message. Interestingly, using a pendulum with a spirit board wouldn't be unlike the divination technique described in Marcellinus's writing (mentioned in Chapter 1).

ASK THE GLASS/SPIRIT OF THE GLASS/ THE MOVING WINEGLASS

This is an improvised talking board game, in which players use an upturned glass and the letters of the alphabet arranged in a circle (such as by being written on a piece of paper). The earliest known mention of this game was found in a do-it-yourself article printed in a Spiritualist magazine from 1911, but it could be older.

The object is much the same as a talking board, with the only real difference being that a wineglass is used instead of a planchette. Growing up, my siblings and I (usually with friends or cousins) would play this game by using an upturned whiskey glass and the wooden tile pieces from Scrabble, arranging the letters in a circle around the glass, allowing ample room for the pieces so that it was clear what letter the glass was indicating. It always felt like there truly was a spirit inside the glass, moving it across the kitchen table. I loved playing this game, and it was especially effective at cementing my status as "the weird kid" at slumber parties when I suggested that we break out a glass and game pieces in order to play.

TABLE TURNING

Table turning is a type of séance that was popular in the late nineteenth century, in which participants would sit around a table, place their hands on it, and wait for the table to tilt or rotate. The alphabet would be slowly spoken aloud, and the table would tilt at the appropriate letter, thus spelling out words and phrases. Most of it was likely due to the ideomotor response, but there were a number of frauds who would actively trick people with this (and similar) techniques.

Table turning was one of the precursors of the talking board, evolving to make use of letters and numbers that are easier to communicate.

KOKKURI

There are two versions of kokkuri, a Japanese divination game. It was originally similar to table turning. The older technique, which isn't practiced as commonly today, used a small table supported by three bamboo rods. The surface was usually covered with a cloth, upon which participants would lay

their hands. Depending on what the spirits were communicating, their hands would shift around.

Similar to how table turning evolved into the talking board, kokkuri saw a similar evolution, eventually becoming a piece of paper or card with kanji (Japanese characters) written on it, with a coin used in place of a planchette.

Kokkuri-san is the being that is said to be summoned when one plays kokkuri. The spirit is a cross between a fox, a dog, and a raccoon. The name "kokkuri" combines syllables from the Japanese words for each animal.

CHARLIE CHARLIE

Charlie Charlie is the game that is perhaps the most similar to a pendulum, at least in its overall simplicity. It is a modern variation of a Spanish game called *Juego de la Lapicera* ("The Pencil Game"), and became popular in the English-speaking world after the hashtag #CharlieCharlieChallenge went viral in 2015.

The game is quite simple, with two variations. An earlier version of the game requires two players and four pencils, but there is very little information about this much less common version (but it is believed to employ the ideomotor response). The version of the game that became the most popular, however, only requires two pencils and a piece of paper. One pencil sits on top of the other, so that the two pencils intersect, forming a grid.

The pencils are placed on top of a piece of paper, on which either "YES" or "NO" is written in the upper right and lower left "quadrants" and the other is written in the upper left and lower right, so that when the top pencil moves, it will point to either the YES or the NO. The player asks "Charlie" a question, and the pencil moves to point to its answer. The pencil likely moves from outside stimuli like the breath of the person or persons playing, or a breeze, or some other external factor—perhaps even the pull of gravity.

The game went viral on the internet, with satirical websites claiming that five hundred people had died by suicide after playing this game. Like so many internet crazes, the satire was lost on the majority of people, so this fed into a panic around the game, leading to countries banning it outright.

Charlie Charlie is ultimately like Bloody Mary or other childhood games—a pervasive, slightly spooky legend that most people don't believe in, but that can still stir up hysteria under the right conditions.

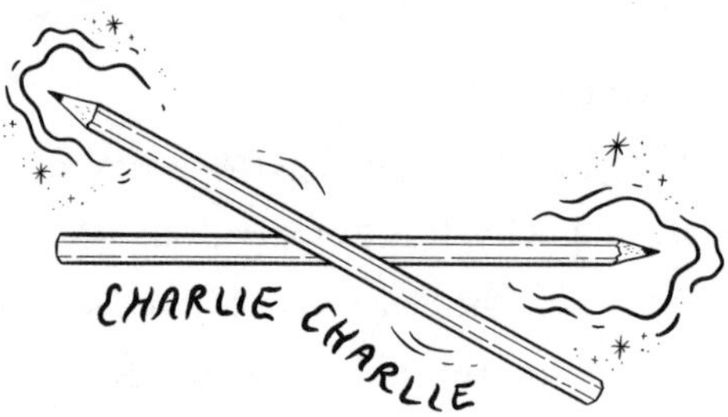

Hypnotism

There's a Pokémon called Hypno. It's a Psychic type, typically yellow and white, with pointed ears and a long nose, depicted holding a pendulum in its hand. Its abilities include Insomnia, Inner Focus, and Forewarn (the latter two are actually very astute for something involving a pendulum). Hypno is just one of many examples of pop culture using a pendulum-like item in conjunction with hypnotism.

Movies, television, and comic books often have depictions of a hypnotist who dresses in a top hat and a black cape, wielding a pocket watch or a suspended charm decorated with a black and white spiral. This hypnotist, looking like the magician from the 1970 film *The Wizard of Gore,* will lull someone into a state of somnambulism by using their pendulum to hypnotize the poor unsuspecting victim. Other times, the hypnotist will be less nefarious, either failing completely, or convincing someone to act like a chicken when they hear a particular sound or trigger word.

In reality, hypnosis rarely, if ever, uses a pendulum. Hypnosis works by having the subject enter into a heightened state of concentration and focus, causing them to become more suggestable. There is some argument to be made that one could more easily hypnotize themselves by using a pendulum, but similar effects could be achieved by concentrating on any repetitive pattern. Stage magicians who practice hypnosis achieve what they do by just playing into the fact that the subject is already agreeable and willing to be hypnotized. You'll rarely, if ever, see them using a pocket watch as a pendulum to lull someone into an altered state of consciousness. Not to mention that most magicians don't dress in top hats or capes anymore.

Chapter 4

HERMETICISM AND PENDULUMS

The Kybalion is a book first published by the Yogi Publication Society of Chicago in 1908, purported to be written by a collection of sages known only as the Three Initiates (though there are now very reasonable theories as to who actually wrote the book). *The Kybalion* is presented as an introduction to an ancient mystical practice, previously passed down from teacher to student by oral tradition. (For more information on the book, read the *The Kybalion: Centenary Edition* published by TarcherPerigee, or watch the documentary hosted by Mitch Horowitz.) *The Kybalion* includes a section of the Seven Hermetic Principles. These principles are:

* The Principle of Mentalism
* The Principle of Correspondence
* The Principle of Vibration
* The Principle of Polarity
* The Principle of Rhythm
* The Principle of Cause and Effect
* The Principle of Gender

Presented as a philosophy that could be applied to day-to-day life, provided that the individual is open and willing to receive and hear it, these principles are related within the pages of the book.

The principles, as well as a great deal of *The Kybalion* as a whole, draw comparisons to New Thought and positive thought philosophies. While I won't be getting into these too much, it is pertinent to discuss Hermeticism and the Seven Principles within the context of pendulums. Some theorists claim that there is a direct relationship between pendulums and Hermetic tradition. This is an example of the unreliable narrator we see consistently in the metaphysical space, especially on the internet, discussed in Chapter 2.

As far as I can find, there is no strong link between Hermeticism and pendulums, divinatory or otherwise. The link appears to have manifested because of the Seven Hermetic Principles, and in particular, the Principle of Rhythm. These types of incorrect connections seem to be fairly consistent in the internet age. I was a bit irritated when I realized that yet another pendulum connection that others have made was likely because of misreading and misinterpreting information. Hermeticism is already riddled with pseudo-historic ideas that loop in real and imagined historical ideas, in a realm that is already quite broad and nonspecific. "Hermetic" can feel like a pretty big umbrella term, and that's because it actually is. This isn't to say that Hermeticism isn't something ancient or relevant. A lot of valuable information can be found within Hermeticism, and a great deal of Hermeticism acts as a root and offers source material for modern occultism and metaphysics, and magic as a whole. Hermetic tradition is deeply integrated and woven into a lot of contemporary metaphysical practices and ideas. It's almost impossible to escape it. But—it is not directly related to the history of pendulums. No more so than Wicca or

Christianity or even the work of Galileo (who has the greatest claim to relevancy here, although his focus was certainly not the magical).

Still, in reading *The Kybalion* to provide context to what I was seeing, and confirm that I wasn't missing anything, I did find that a few of the principles do lend themselves rather prudently to the magic of pendulums.

THE PRINCIPLE OF VIBRATION

"Nothing rests; everything moves; everything vibrates."

—***THE KYBALION***

The Principle of Vibration points to a physical reality that everything is made of molecules and atomic structures that are never at rest, literally meaning that everything is, in fact, in motion, every second of every day. No matter how solid something may be, its atomic structure is still always in motion, and these states of matter can always change.

For the pendulum, we see this manifest in the ideas around the ideomotor response, and also in the fact that even when a pendulum is at rest, it is never completely still. A pendulum is susceptible to the most minute movements, causing it to move.

THE PRINCIPLE OF POLARITY

"Everything is dull; everything has poles; everything has a pair of opposites; like and unlike are same; opposites are identical in nature, but different in degree; extremes meet; all truths are but half-truths; all paradoxes may be reconciled."

—*THE KYBALION*

While I'm not sure I completely agree with this as a philosophy, there is no doubt that magnets attract as opposites, and each magnet is made up of the same two polarities. A pendulum always returns to center, and the differences in what we perceive as "yes/no/maybe" are arbitrary, based on our own understanding of opposites and direction.

THE PRINCIPLE OF RHYTHM

"Everything flows, out and in; everything has its tides; all things rise and fall; the pendulum-swing can manifest in everything; the measure of the swing to the right is the measure of the swing to the left; rhythm compensates."

—*THE KYBALION*

This principle speaks directly to the mathematical and physical effects of the pendulum. However, this doesn't mean that there is a direct relationship, and it is more about how we can understand pendulums as a metaphor. As much as it is about rhythm, I think it can be used to understand the concept of balance. This extends to the previous Principle of Polarity, too. Can the pendulum help us understand ideas of balance and returning to our centers on a metaphysical level?

Part 2

PENDULUM CRAFT

Chapter 5

WHY USE A PENDULUM?

For a long time, I really thought that divination was the only use for a pendulum. However, it was only when I began to use this tool in other ways, especially in conjunction with my Reiki and energetic healing practices, that I recognized the pendulum for the game changer that it is. Using a pendulum is a personal experience, and while it can be intensely useful for predictive or determinative practices, you may find yourself gravitating beyond dowsing, divination, and radiesthesia to healing, crafting, or something else. Additionally, each pendulum has its own personality, talents, and downfalls. What works for one person might not work for you, but you may also discover an incredibly unique use for a pendulum that is entirely your own.

So, why use a pendulum? I don't think that there's one simple answer to that question. Why use any magical tool? If you feel called to the pendulum, there's a reason for it. That reason might not make itself known immediately, but magical tools call out to you because they're going to fill a purpose in your life, and in your craft. When you think *this speaks to me*, that's because there's already a link between you and that tool, present because of ancestral knowledge, a connection to the path you're on, messages from guides, or any other reason under the moon and stars. Use a pendulum because you feel called to it. Experiment, meditate, explore, play. The relationship you're meant to have with that pendulum will make itself clear as time moves on. Before you know it, you'll understand exactly why you picked up that pendulum, and why it was meant to be part of your craft.

Some of these uses are frivolous, and many people warn against using pendulums for frivolity, but I don't really agree with this. What is frivolity? Why can't magic be frivolous? Not everything needs to be serious all the time. Not to mention what's frivolous or silly to one person can be very helpful to another. For example, I included "fidget tool" as one of the uses for a pendulum. I included this because I'm a neurodivergent witch, and I will play with everything and anything on hand as a way of stimming or helping myself focus. ("Stimming" refers to "self-stimulation"—repetitive actions or behaviors common in people with autism or ADHD as a way to regulate emotions or show excitement, or just because it feels good.) I'm sure that a lot of people can relate to this. There's nothing wrong with using a magical tool as a fidget tool (or vice versa!). Magical tools are special, sure, but they're not meant to be precious. They're meant to be used, and that means that you get to decide how to use them. Be silly, be playful, be serious, be whatever you need to do the work. Don't be defined by other people and what they think is right or wrong. You do you!

When it comes to pendulums, I think that as long as you're not flipping haphazardly between topics or uses within the same session, you should be fine. What really matters is focus, intention, and clarity. As long as you're being clear with your intentions and how you're wording questions (see Chapter 11), you can use the pendulum for anything you want, at any time. Play and experimentation can help you determine what your relationship with your pendulum is, and how it can best help you in your journey.

77 Uses for a Pendulum

1. Asking for advice
2. Contacting spirits
3. Connecting with guides
4. Meditation
5. Crystal healing
6. General healing
7. Body scanning
8. Chakra balancing/unblocking
9. Deciding on what herb to use in a spell
10. Finding the right crystal
11. Making a schedule
12. Choosing an outfit
13. Deciding on what to make for dinner
14. Finding lost things
15. Selecting the best magical tool
16. Finding a tarot card
17. Making art
18. Energetic healing on an animal
19. Energetic healing on a plant
20. Determining whether a crystal needs to be cleansed or charged
21. Deciding on the best lunar phase to work with
22. Determining the best planetary time to work in
23. Self-work
24. Shadow work
25. Deciding on a new tarot deck
26. Determining if something will be a good purchase or not
27. Finding the best produce at a grocery store
28. Deciding on the best gem essence or tincture to take
29. Deciding on a new routine for day-to-day
30. Focusing on what project to work on
31. Prioritizing tasks
32. Connecting with your creative side
33. Reading your body
34. Health diagnoses (**Note:** this can give you an idea, but it should not replace medical advice or treatments)
35. Aligning with planets
36. Getting to know your subconscious
37. Dream interpretation
38. Clearing a space

39. Clearing the energetic self/ aura
40. Choosing the best color for a space
41. Feng shui
42. Amusing your cats
43. Focusing energy
44. Manifesting
45. Cleansing a crystal
46. Charging a crystal
47. Choosing a path or direction
48. Determining the best career path (or what to do next in your career)
49. Choosing a topic to write about
50. Connecting with ancestors
51. Connecting with deities
52. Determining if a space is haunted
53. Defining or clarifying emotions
54. Deciding where to travel
55. Putting your needs or wants into words
56. Clearing magical tools
57. Praying
58. Determining if something is beneficial to you
59. Calming yourself
60. A fidget tool
61. A necklace or pendant
62. Something to play with while waiting on the phone with the bank
63. Charging a sigil
64. Determining the best time for something
65. Clearing your thoughts
66. Casting a magic circle
67. Charging a cup of tea or coffee
68. Dowsing
69. Carving a sigil or a petition into a candle
70. Bibliomancy
71. Deciding how to decorate a space
72. Glamour magic (deciding on what makeup to wear that day, charging brushes, etc.)
73. Deciding on what to do on a date
74. Channeling information
75. Having fun with physics
76. Charging ingredients while baking or cooking
77. Determining what you need to let go of

Chapter 6

CHOOSING A PENDULUM

There is no right or wrong way to choose a pendulum. There are a lot of factors and variables, but I see a pendulum as any other magical tool. It is a tool, but it is also an ally, an inanimate familiar. It is a tool for you to extend and focus your own energy, to help you get the information and guidance you need. Early ceremonial magic set the tone that we need props and decoration to make magic happen. This isn't true. You are capable of magic and focusing your energy without the add-ons. *But*, those add-ons, like tools and spell ingredients and even the right garb, can help you get there easier and faster. The kind of information and healing you can access by using a pendulum is already available to you, but using a pendulum can help channel it into a language that you can more easily interpret and understand.

Like I said, there is no right or wrong way to choose a pendulum. I've walked into all kinds of witch shops and purchased pendulums simply because I connected with them for some unknown reason. Sometimes it was because there was something about the shape and material that resonated with me. Or I would notice one pendulum swinging on a display, when all the others were completely still. After a lot of experimentation, I now know that anything will do in a pinch, but there are some pendulums that are better suited to certain tasks and functions. But even that can change depending on the individual operating the pendulum.

The key is to trust your gut and your intuition. You can do all the research in the world and still not get the answer that you actually need. All you can do is trust and try. You might get really lucky and find a pendulum that fits every purpose you might need. You might find yourself with a small collection of pendulums after you notice that they're not one-size-fits-all tools, and each one is better suited to a specific task. And if you find a pendulum you like, you're not committed to that pendulum forever.

If you're feeling called to seek out a pendulum, but you're not sure where to start, you can use this book to find what materials or shapes would be more ideal to your purposes. You can be analytical about it, but you can also just go into a witch shop and look at the pendulums and see what resonates. You can also ask the pendulum itself! Say aloud or in your head, "Are you the pendulum for me?" Then pay attention to its movements. Notice how it makes you feel. When you pick up the pendulum, how does it feel in your hand? How does it make your body feel? Try different pendulums until you find that right fit.

MAGICAL MATERIALS

There are many materials that can be used to make pendulums (or to choose from). Different materials such as wood, stone, metal, or plastic will offer different benefits or detriments, depending on what you are using it for or who is using it. Some materials are more common because they are practical, while some may offer unique benefits for individuals, depending on variables like your astrological chart.

Nowadays, most pendulums are made of crystal stones, but metals and wood are not uncommon. Of all of the pendulums I have in my collection, my favorite is a metal one made of steel, a metal alloy. When choosing a pendulum, personal taste should be seriously considered. If the physical form of your pendulum does not connect with you—its texture, vibration, color—this can cause a feeling of unease to develop around the item. Magical tools are, above all, most dependent on their connection to the user. So if you're physically "trying out" new pendulums, focus on what resonates with you based on touch and feel. And if you're ordering online, keep this chapter on hand.

When selecting a material for a pendulum, you can basically use anything. You can even use a found object, provided it can be suspended from a string or chain. In a pinch, a necklace with a pendant, or a ring hung from a string, can serve as a very practical and functional pendulum. I have removed a necklace from my neck and used it to help make decisions when I'm in a particularly stressful or difficult situation. Sometimes you just need an objective third party that can help decide on something mundane. I believe I used my makeshift pendulum to determine whether my spouse and I should see the *Barbie* movie or not. *THAT* level of mundanity.

Some schools of thought around pendulums (especially in the realms of radiesthesia) insist that the pendulum must be crafted from natural materials, with a special focus on metals like gold, silver, brass, or copper. Aside from the potential expense, all are fine choices, but I do believe that some would be better choices than others. The real key is to find a material that you like and that feels good. Everything else is secondary, because at the end of the day, we are all completely unique beings with unique vibrations and auras, and different materials may react with us differently. We may react to certain materials differently than others do. You may have a metal allergy, or be especially sensitive to certain types of stones or metals. You should take these kinds of factors into account when making your selection.

On plastic and human-made materials: It is my belief that all that exists is of nature, even if it was created in a lab. Just because something may not grow in the woods doesn't mean that it's not of the natural world, or that it didn't come from it. We are always part of nature, whether we are living on a self-sustaining farm in the wilderness, or in an apartment in the middle of a city. Separating ourselves from nature only serves to create a hierarchical gap between ourselves and other living things. I choose to recognize everything as having meaning within the context of nature and the outside world. This is a very animist approach to the world, but I feel like it does deepen the magic and the intention for me.

Woods

All of the following woods/plants were (and are) commonly used for divination, particularly dowsing, and could be used to craft a wand or a pendulum. If the correspondence and meanings resonate with you, consider commissioning an artist to craft a custom tool for you.

HAZEL

Luck / creation / creativity / protection / love
Crown chakra / Libra, Aquarius / Mercury

Celtic legends describe the hazelnut as an emblem of concentrated wisdom. The nut is nutrition for the body and the soul. Hazel wood is a great material for a pendulum, and you could even make one from the nut itself.

It might not have the most longevity (nuts do spoil!), but it would be the right kind of shape.

USE A HAZEL PENDULUM FOR:

* creative endeavors
* channeling wisdom and helpful messages
* guidance around uncertainties

WITCH HAZEL

Protection / healing / divination
Heart, crown chakras / Taurus / Sun

Witch hazel is one of my favorite magical plants. It is very practical (to the point that you can find witch hazel astringents in most first aid sections of grocery stores or pharmacies). Witch hazel is said to have gotten its name because of its history of being used for divination. It is healing, protective, and carries intense dark moon energy (despite traditionally being ruled by the Sun).

Witch hazel helps mend broken hearts and is good for cuts and bites. Most plants that heal and soothe the physical body can also be used to heal and soothe the emotional, mental, and spiritual selves, and witch hazel is no different.

USE A WITCH HAZEL PENDULUM FOR:

* body healing
* clearing spaces and auras
* general divination

PEACH

Protection / healing / exorcism / creativity / creation / Venus energy
Heart, sacral chakras / Libra, Taurus, Cancer / Venus, Moon

In China, the peach branch is used to drive away evil spirits, and so it is hung outside of homes during the lunar new year to invite good luck and longevity, as well as to protect the home from unwanted spirits. The entire peach tree, from the branches to the fruit to the pits, is used to call in protection. Shinto and Taoist beliefs hold the peach as significant and sacred.

Ruled by Venus, the peach can help oppose any negative effects or influences of Mars. If you are someone with heavy Venus influences on your natal chart, you may struggle when the current astrological forecast is showing strong Martian energy. This may be uncomfortable for you. Perhaps working with peach would soothe your tender heart.

Peach wood (or a pendulum made out of a peach pit) could prove to be a helpful tool and a strong ally for anyone with major Venusian placements, especially Taurus or Libra moons.

USE A PEACH PENDULUM FOR:

* clearing energies and spaces
* determining if a space or body needs clearing or unblocking
* balancing energies

APPLE

Love / healing / transformation / knowledge / secret knowledge / hidden secrets / growth / unicorn magic / health
Heart, sacral chakras / Scorpio, Capricorn / Pluto, Saturn, Moon

The apple tree is an ally when looking for answers and information. It is a plant of divination and transformation, conjuring Scorpian energy in its wake. Apple is especially potent around love divination and love spells, but one must approach such magic with the utmost caution, unless they are self-love spells, or spells being used to strengthen an existing relationship (and you have the consent of all involved). Matters of the heart are delicate, and should not be approached with any frivolity, especially when magic is involved.

Apple is also a necromantic plant, with close connections to death, Samhain, and immortality. Ancient Irish law saw death as a suitable punishment for cutting down an apple tree.

Apple wood makes suitable and potent magic wands, and would make a good pendulum, too, especially if one is seeking to do divination around the time of Samhain, or around themes of transformation.

USE AN APPLE WOOD PENDULUM FOR:

* guidance
* accessing secret knowledge
* channeling spirits
* general divination

Witch Tip

Any materials or ingredients that correspond to transformation can be utilized for beautiful and divine magic or meditation around being transgender, or transitioning. If you are trans, whether you are transitioning or not, transformational plants and minerals and allies can benefit you and support you in your journey. For example, if you're a trans woman or trans femme, you might find a lot of support from apple because of the Venusian energy. A trans man or transmasc individual could find support through a Mars-ruled plant. A nonbinary individual could get support from Mercury-ruled transformative plants.

WILLOW

Divination / crafting / creativity / protection / lunar magic / communicating with spirits / necromancy / death rites + death magic / transformation
Root chakra / Scorpio / Pluto, Moon

Willow is associated with death and witches. It is a triple goddess/goddex plant, resonating closely and fully with every aspect of the Moon. It protects against unwanted energy (especially what some might call "evil" or "negative"). The tree is said to make the best of all ritual wands, especially when it is used to create magic wands dedicated to lunar magic. The wood carries a lot of strong energy, making it a good choice for crafting many different witches' tools. Willow can be used as an ally when conjuring or communicating with spirits, especially the deceased. Willow is magic, and generally more than happy to aid magical practitioners of any kind.

Sacred to Hekate, and any deity connected to the underworld, willow is connected to the journey to the beyond, aiding in ensuring a safe journey to the underworld. It is said that if you plant a willow and it (or a direct descendant born through a cutting) is alive when you die, it will protect your soul when it leaves your body.

Willow is a tree of enchantment. It can charge a rock crystal with healing and protective abilities.

USE A WILLOW PENDULUM FOR:

* general divination
* connecting with spirits
* clearing spaces and auras
* clearing and charging crystals

DOGWOOD

Protection / hidden information / keeping secrets / canine magic
Throat, heart chakras / Taurus, Leo / Saturn, Mercury

Dogwood's special talent is being able to keep secrets and help individuals keep a cool head. It's a plant that can help you maintain composure when discussing difficult topics with difficult people. It can also help you keep an open mind. If you are going into a meeting where you need to maintain confidence and clarity, dogwood can be a good ally. In divination, dogwood can help you trust yourself and your intuition.

Dogwood can keep meetings and correspondences secret. This includes private writings, such as a diary or a grimoire. Dogwood will protect your secrets. An oil or an essence made from dogwood flowers can be used to anoint a letter, sealing it and ensuring that the contents will be kept until the intended recipient opens it.

Dogwood is protective. Trust dogwood the way you would an entrusted guard dog.

USE A DOGWOOD PENDULUM FOR:

* accessing secret knowledge
* finding lost things
* dowsing
* sealing grimoires and other magical tomes that you wish to keep private and hidden

BEECH

Revealing truths / inspiration / guidance / creativity / muse / lunar magic
Crown, third eye chakras / Libra, Aquarius / Sun, Mercury

Beech is a patron of the creative process, and it loves being interacted with in creative ways. It is a literary muse and can be carried to increase creative powers. When placed in a book (such as a journal or diary), beech will aid in providing inspiration, especially for those creating new rituals or magical literature. The ways to invoke the literary and creative powers of beech are only limited by one's own imagination.

USE A BEECH PENDULUM FOR:

* the creative process
* gaining inspiration
* personal messages and guidance

MAPLE

Nourishment / abundance / love / money
Heart chakra / Taurus / Venus

Branches of the maple make very suitable wands. The leaves can be used in love spells and money spells. The sweetness attracts abundance.

USE A MAPLE PENDULUM FOR:

* charging magical items and crystals for abundance spells
* receiving loving messages
* enchanting or charging meals and ingredients

Metals

Metal is a physical representation of alchemy that makes itself known almost every day, present in everything from tools to jewelry to electronic devices. We can mark human evolution by when we learned to work with different metals. For something that is so deeply connected to the mundane world, metals from iron to silver to gold are very magical.

IRON

Protection / psychic armor / clearing / practicality
Root chakra / Capricorn, Aries / Mars, Earth

The process of forging iron for tools and weapons was starting to be mastered in Eurasia during the 2nd millennium BCE, with the Iron Age starting around 1200 BCE, when iron started to displace the use of copper alloys. In folklore around the world (especially in Eurasia), iron is believed to be a metal that protects against witches, evil spirits, faeries, and other unwanted supernatural beings. Why do you think people hang iron horseshoes above their doors? If you have seen the TV show *Supernatural*, you may remember the Winchester brothers using iron filings and salt to defend themselves against ghosts and other spooky monsters. This is grounded in real folklore, and the combination would be a formidable defense against such entities (but please—don't go filling gun shells with salt and iron filings). The portrayal of iron as protective is likely connected to the fact that iron was used to form weapons and armor, but there might also be a simple connection to the fact that iron must be forged and shaped by fire, and across a lot of cultures nothing is considered more purifying than fire.

In *The Golden Bough,* James George Frazer discusses how some cultures consider iron to be tabooed, calling it "obnoxious" (earlier definitions of the word "obnoxious" mean hurtful or injurious). The metal was forbidden from ancient Greek and Roman temples. Frazer suggests that because the metal was seen as dangerous and humans didn't want to approach it, spirits or ghosts wouldn't want to approach it, either.

Prior to smithing and forging iron from ore, some ancient civilizations found ways to form meteoric iron into ceremonial items. Nineteen meteoric iron objects were found in Tutankhamun's tomb, including a dagger. Created during the Bronze Age, iron items like these were deemed so rare and difficult to craft that they were reserved for people of high status and were considered more valuable than gold.

Iron is a good conductor because its metallic bonds have electrons that are free to move around more than one atom. Not only does it mean that it can conduct electricity, but it can also conduct energy and vibrations. Iron is fairly neutral in terms of energetic vibration, allowing it to channel other energy quite favorably. Still, iron is magnetic, meaning it will soak up the energy from other sources (including whoever is holding it), so it's prudent to cleanse it regularly. Fortunately, iron is cleansed easily and quickly by using common materials like household salt or the Sun. One should note that iron, especially pure iron, is prone to oxidation (rust), so do keep your iron pendulum away from water, or be prepared to care for it to prevent rusting. The metal in most commercially available pendulums are likely to be alloys like stainless steel, so rust isn't normally much of an issue.

Iron and iron pendulums are beneficial for cleansing spaces, clearing energy, and attracting and removing energy. An iron pendulum will not be the best choice for communicating with spirits. The superstitions around iron do come from somewhere, so why take the chance if your goal is to speak to spirits and entities?

Common irons and iron alloys include cast iron, steel, stainless steel, surgical stainless steel, and wrought iron. There are many others, varying in specificity and uses.

USE AN IRON OR IRON ALLOY PENDULUM FOR:

* cleansing or clearing spaces and energies
* cleansing and charging crystals
* charging magical tools and spell ingredients

NICKEL

Clearing / protection / attraction
Root chakra / Capricorn, Sagittarius / Mars

Nickel is a very common metal, appearing in several alloys. The use of nickel as a metal can be traced back to 3500 BCE, where it appeared as a natural meteoric nickel-iron alloy that was used to craft some items (the nickel percentage is relatively low, but still present). Nickel is ferromagnetic, meaning that it is strongly attracted to magnets, and can become magnetic.

Because of its magnetic nature, nickel can attract energy to it. If it's being used in a magical context, nickel requires regular clearing and/or cleansing. Similar to iron, its magnetic qualities make it a good material to cleanse and clear spaces and energetic bodies by gathering energy and removing them. This ability is not discerning, so it will completely neutralize the energy of a space, removing both the bad/unwanted energy and the good. It's essential to welcome in wanted energy afterward by burning incense or calling in helpful spirits.

USE A NICKEL PENDULUM FOR:

* clearing or cleansing spaces and energies
* neutralizing energies

ALUMINUM

Reflection / introspection / attraction
Crown, third eye chakras / Aquarius, Pisces / Moon, Venus

Visually similar to silver, aluminum has a lower density than other common metals. Apparently, aluminum is not widely recommended for pendulums. According to occult writer Raymond Buckland, aluminum is manufactured in such a way that it is disruptive to most auric fields. However, aluminum is a naturally forming element, so I think there's more to it.

Aluminum is reflective, and reflective surfaces tend to have magical potential. They need to be cleansed regularly because they can trap energy, for better or for worse. Because of this ability to hold onto energy, aluminum could be a good way to ensure that a pendulum is yours and only yours, allowing for hyper-personal readings and insights.

Corundum is the crystalline form of aluminum oxide (a chemical compound of aluminum and oxygen), and the most common natural formation of the compound. Corundum crystals include rubies and sapphires. I don't know if Buckland knew this when he was so quick to dismiss aluminum as a magical material. Aluminum oxide was also used in alchemy, referred to as aluminum salts in several texts.

For the sake of science, I made a pendulum out of aluminum foil. I shaped the foil into a pendulum shape, using a pair of pliers to compress and shape the metal until I was satisfied. I folded part of the metal into a handle shape and attached a piece of string (fairly thin and light mercerized cotton). I was not displeased with the result. It worked well and performed well under the usual tests I run to determine whether I like something as a pendulum. In a pinch, I think it would be as good as any other metal, especially for divination and cleansing materials and tools.

USE AN ALUMINUM PENDULUM FOR:

* personal readings and self-work, especially around personal reflection and introspection
* divination
* cleansing materials and tools

GOLD

Money / abundance / amplifier / magnifier / reflection
Solar plexus chakra / Leo, Aries / Sun

Gold is a precious metal, appearing throughout human history. It has been described as a symbol of wealth in folklore and mythology for thousands of years. Magically and energetically, gold is a magnifier. Ruled by the Sun and Leo, gold is highly conductive, so it allows the transmission and passage of energy. If someone is already energetically sensitive, they may wish to avoid gold because it could be overwhelming. Gold heightens emotions and energy, boosting already positive feelings, but doing the same for negative or difficult emotions. If you feel happy, gold will magnify that. If you're feeling sad, gold will make you feel worse.

Gold may not be the best choice for a pendulum, unless you are specifically dowsing for gold (like attracts like). If you are using a gold pendulum for divination, you may find difficulty discerning or interpreting what is being reflected back, or what is being indicated to you during the reading. Gold is fickle, and a lot of stories about gold end in tragedy for a reason. Plus, it is rather expensive, which is okay for some, but I think it's better to find a useful tool that has practical applications for you and your purposes.

USE A GOLD PENDULUM FOR:

* charging materials and ingredients for abundance spells
* receiving messages and insight
* accessing information, like the Akashic records
* boosting or amplifying energy

SILVER

Emotions / psychic gifts / intuition / protection / purifying
Crown, third eye chakras / Pisces, Cancer / Moon

Silver is highly conductive, but it is ruled by the Moon, so it has a serene and calming energy. Its lunar rulings also make it a useful tool for tapping into one's intuition and psychic abilities. Silver has the ability to purify and cleanse more efficiently than other metals. The folklore surrounding silver is similar to iron, especially in the sense that it can be used for protection. Think about how silver is said to burn vampires and kill werewolves.

Silver allows for the transmission of information without getting weighed down by exterior energy or vibrations. Like other metals that are not magnetic (which is most metals in day-to-day situations for the average individual), silver won't hold onto energy quite as much as something that is magnetic. Silver is also naturally purifying.

USE A SILVER PENDULUM FOR:

* clearing and cleansing spaces and energies
* accessing information and guidance
* readings in which you need to access your intuition and psychic gifts

COPPER

Protection / psychic armor / connecting with ancestors / past lives / clearing / cleansing
Heart chakra / Taurus, Sagittarius / Venus

Copper is a material that, arguably, unites large swaths of human history. It is soft, malleable, and has so many useful qualities: as currency, as a tool, as an adornment. It was the first metal to be used by humans, and examples of early copper metallurgy are found around the world. Early uses of metal go back to the Neolithic Age, over 10,000 years ago, leading to the Chalcolithic Age (approximately 6,500 years ago), which was marked by an increased use of smelting and metallurgy.

Copper is a fascinating metal. It has a high thermal conductivity, and high electrical conductivity. It is one of the few metals that can be found in nature in a usable form. Copper has been used in art, building materials, and science (including medical science). It is essential to all living organisms because it is a component of an enzyme. It is biostatic, so bacteria and other forms of life can't grow on it. Copper has been used to facilitate faster telecommunications and faster transmission of data. It's just a cool metal that is both ancient and modern, holding almost infinite possibilities and uses.

In the realm of the magical and metaphysical, copper is ruled by Venus (a correspondence assigned in ancient Rome because of the goddess as well as the titular planet's brightness) and has as many magical uses as it has practical uses. Its aesthetic and utilitarian qualities, coupled with its conductivity, mean that it's capable of most magical applications, including protection magic, clearing, cleansing, offering support, assisting in channeling information, and more. Copper has a soft and supportive energy. As a pendulum, it has a lot of potential to be a powerful ally, but one that is not overly intense in its vibration or energy.

Copper alloys carry similar energies, but aren't quite as powerful in their capabilities. However, a brass or bronze pendulum would offer similar traits in terms of divination and magic.

USE A COPPER PENDULUM FOR:

* receiving strong messages and guidance
* clearing and cleansing spaces and energy
* charging protective stones, talismans, and anything else that might be used for protection magic
* connecting to ancestors and past lives

Lead

Protection / shapeshifting / divination
Root chakra / Capricorn, Scorpio / Saturn

Ruled by Saturn, lead is not as commonly used as it once was, due to its toxicity. Lead is a metal that was very present in antiquity, due largely in part to its low melting point, which would have made it easier to acquire and work with. Nowadays, it is not recommended to use lead for any tools, magical or otherwise. But it is a metal that comes up in magical and historical writing, so I'm including it for the sake of completeness and relevance. Lead was a common material for making tools, including plumb bobs, because of its low melting point. In fact, because lead is so easily melted, there was a type of divination called molybdomancy, which involved dropping molten lead into water and then interpreting the shapes that formed. This is similar to carromancy, which follows the same principle, but uses hot wax from candles instead of lead.

USE A LEAD PENDULUM FOR:

* general divination

Due to toxicity this is not a recommended material for your pendulum, but I include it here due to its prevalence in antiquity.

PEWTER

Protection / house magic / practical magic
Heart chakra / Libra, Pisces / Moon, Venus

Pewter is a metal alloy that consists of tin, antimony, copper, bismuth, and sometimes silver. In antiquity, pewter was made with lead to act as a hardener alongside (or sometimes instead of) copper and antimony. Pewter was a very common metal for decorative and household purposes. You are unlikely to find a pewter pendulum today, but should you find or craft one, you may find that it has a soft and neutral energy. Vibrationally, pewter might not pick up on much in terms of energy or information, but due to its complex nature, it may surprise you in how it heals and guides you.

USE A PEWTER PENDULUM FOR:

* gentle inner work and healing
* receiving gentle and helpful guidance

Crystals and Stones

The most common pendulums are made of crystal and stone. If you peruse the internet, you'll find that some people suggest that it's because crystals already exist at a higher frequency and have their own high vibration. I'm not convinced that this is necessarily a positive in terms of divination and pendulum use. Some vibrations and energies can be overpowering, and not every crystal or stone will be beneficial to every user. Ultimately, you'll want something neutral and natural for your pendulum. Some crystals or stones are naturally better suited to this purpose than others. This section is not intended to dissuade you from using a pendulum that speaks to you. The initial intuitive response you have to a tool will always be the best deciding factor. But consider the following information if you're particularly drawn to a crystal or stone and want to use it as a guide, to help you find one best suited for the kind of task you'd like to perform with your pendulum.

AMETHYST

Intuition / psychic gifts / protection / transmuting
Third eye, crown chakras / Aquarius, Pisces / Jupiter, Neptune

Amethyst is a protective stone with buoyant energy, and a great ally for anxious or sensitive witches. Amethyst is one of the more common stones used in pendulums, and for a good reason. It is gentle, but also capable of heightening intuition, bringing out psychic gifts, and helping you achieve higher levels of consciousness and vibrations (if you're into that kind of thing).

Amethyst is a good option for someone living in a large urban area, especially in an apartment building or dorm, as it can guard against geopathic and environmental stress. Amethyst's ability to neutralize and transmute energy makes it a good stone to have in the home as well, especially in a place that gets a lot of visitors.

USE AN AMETHYST PENDULUM FOR:

* purifying a space or energy
* body scanning and healing
* introspection and self-work

Witch Tip

Did you find a crystal that you love, but it's not quite doing what you need? Try programming it! "Programming" is another word for charging or activating a crystal. Essentially, you are telling the crystal what you need or want it to do, and then giving it the power to do that by offering an energy source (such as sunlight, moonlight, or your own energy through physical touch). Crystals are more suited to some jobs than others, but they are malleable and flexible, with a love for healing and helping. Most crystals are capable of many tasks, even if they're predisposed to something specific. For example, rose quartz is LOVE. It radiates love. It offers love. It just is *love.* All forms of love. It's also sensitive, soft, caring, and compassionate. So if you want to use a rose quartz to cleanse a space, it could be more than capable of doing so. It would simply leave its own energy in its wake, leaving gentle loving energy while removing anything difficult or unwanted.

We all react differently to *everything*, based on our DNA, conditioning, upbringing, astrology, and other factors that make up who we are. In the same way, some crystals will click more, and you can use them any way you see fit.

JASPER (*any kind*)

Power / inspiration / encouragement / support
Root chakra / Aries, Leo / Mars

Jasper is a stone of power and vitality: supportive, inspiring, and motivating. It is sometimes called a "supreme nurturer" because of its ability to gently offer encouragement and support. There are many variations of jasper (including bloodstone), and they are all fiery caretakers, reminding you to have fun without worrying about the details, and telling you that you're doing a good job.

If you need some "you can do it" energy, jasper is a good choice.

USE A JASPER PENDULUM FOR:

* day planning, including determining a direction for the day
* guidance and encouragement

RED JASPER

Guidance / grounding / calming
Root chakra / Aries, Leo

Red jasper, despite being fiery, is a grounding and calming stone. It helps facilitate smooth communication when there are difficult topics to discuss, and it can even help illuminate problems before they become unmanageable. It may help you recognize difficult truths. Red jasper is that aggressive and forceful Aries friend who is loyal to a fault and who just wants the best for you.

USE A RED JASPER PENDULUM FOR:

* supportive guidance
* reality checks
* self-healing journeys

BLUE JASPER

Intuition / inspiration / communication / spirits
Throat chakra / Pisces

The dreamiest of the jaspers, blue jasper taps into Piscean energies, facilitating the flow of words and ideas. It allows clear, smooth communication. Blue jasper also offers a connection to the spiritual realm.

USE A BLUE JASPER PENDULUM FOR:

* communication with the spirit realm
* receiving clear messages from other sources, or yourself
* connecting with guides, deities, ancestors, or others in Spirit

BROWN JASPER

Return to nature / introspection / past lives / ancestors / grounding
Root chakra / Capricorn, Taurus

Brown jasper is deeply connected to the Earth, and is a valuable ally for anyone wishing to deepen their connection with Mother Earth and nature, while also deepening their connection with themselves. Brown jasper aids in meditation, and offers space to connect with past lives. Its connection to the Earth also allows ecological awareness, and helps soothe geopathic and environmental stressors (see sidebar below). It is a great stone for someone in an urban area who has trouble cutting away the noise and energetic overwhelm of living in such an active area.

USE A BROWN JASPER PENDULUM FOR:

* meditation
* connecting to past lives
* introspection and self-work

Geopathic Stress

"Fox, you have mentioned geopathic and environmental stress a couple of times now. What do you mean by that?" Geopathic stress may sound a little scary, but I assure you, it's really not. Geopathic stress is the idea that the Earth has a natural vibration, and that it can be disrupted by natural and man-made underground features. Things like tunnels, sewers, geological faults, pipes, mineral deposits, utility lines, and underground water are all examples of this. Dowsing can be used to determine the presence of these stressors and locate them. Environmental stressors are things occurring in the environment that affect us. There's no real evidence that either geopathic or environmental stressors can affect us, but I do believe that energies and vibrations can affect us. Whether or not you believe in geopathic stressors is up to you. We all feel things differently and are affected differently by things in our environments. The Earth and man-made variables do affect us, but it can be argued that some people are more sensitive and more affected than others. Some people even express having electronic sickness and can't stand to be near anything electronic or anything with radio waves (or similar invisible waves like Wi-Fi). It's up to the individual to decide how much stock one wishes to put into such factors. Personally, I make choices based on how I feel that certain things affect me. I put black tourmaline near electronics because I do notice a difference. Sometimes it all boils down to "Do what works for YOU."

GREEN JASPER

Healing / soothing / comforting / refocus / balance / reframe
Heart chakra / Taurus, Virgo, Libra

Green jasper aids in healing, especially the release of discomfort. It soothes the heart and offers comfort. Green jasper can also help you refocus by offering some balance. If you've been concentrating on something too much to the detriment of those around you, green jasper will help you prioritize and reframe what's most important. I do not recommend using green jasper for healing others or finding lost objects, as green jasper is more focused on healing one individual: you.

USE A GREEN JASPER PENDULUM FOR:

* individual and personal healing
* planning, prioritizing tasks, and scheduling

PURPLE JASPER

Intuition / psychic gifts / spirits / clarity
Crown chakra / Gemini

Purple jasper is a very spiritual stone, offering connection to higher vibrations and the spiritual realms. Purple jasper can unlock and heighten psychic gifts, as well as sharpen one's intuition. It is also a good stone for receiving and giving information, as it removes contradictions, offers clarity, and cuts through uncertainty.

USE A PURPLE JASPER PENDULUM FOR:

* channeling spirits
* receiving information from other realms

YELLOW JASPER

Protection during physical travel / positive energy
Solar plexus chakra / Sagittarius

Yellow jasper offers protection during spiritual work, as well as physical travel. It channels positive energy to help you feel better physically and emotionally. Yellow jasper is best suited for healing, especially through energetic methods like Reiki, by being held or placed on the solar plexus (which is in the middle of the torso, just above the belly button).

As a pendulum, yellow jasper isn't really suited to being used in readings, but it would be a good tool for healing.

USE A YELLOW JASPER PENDULUM FOR:

* healing
* transmuting energy
* channeling positive messages

BLACK JASPER (*also known as basanite*)

Psychic messages / meditation / guidance
Root chakra / Scorpio

Black jasper is a scrying stone, allowing the holder to enter into a deep altered state of consciousness, and said to conjure prophetic dreams and visions. It is well suited to being held while in a meditative state or while sleeping. While it is ruled by the root chakra, black jasper also activates the crown and the third eye, allowing the holder to open up and receive information. To use black jasper as a pendulum is kind of a "hat on a hat" situation. It could be done, but I don't know if it's really necessary. Black jasper is already good at uncovering truths and information, so there is a possibility that a black jasper pendulum would be overwhelming, to the point of being unclear. Instead, using black jasper as an aid while using a different type of pendulum—for example, clear quartz—could have powerful results, because a stone like quartz is so good at focusing in on the important details.

USE A BLACK JASPER PENDULUM FOR:

* scrying
* accessing dream states, conjuring visions

MOOKAITE (*also known as Australian jasper*)

Balancing / awareness / calming
All chakras, depending on color / Libra, Sagittarius

Mookaite balances inner and outer experiences, making it an affirmative stone for anyone experiencing body or gender dysmorphia. This stone provides a deep calm around new experiences, and helps the holder become aware of all possibilities before helping them choose the right one. Mookaite is a very promising stone for a pendulum because it already holds an awareness of the expanse of choices. Despite this awareness, it is a calming stone, cutting away anxiety and overwhelm surrounding decision-making. Mookaite wishes to help you make the best decisions for you, making it a good contender for a pendulum for individuals who have trouble making choices. Mookaite is here to help you with all of that, whether it is in the form of a pendulum or not. It would also be a good ally to have on hand while doing a pendulum reading, because it will help remove any stress or fear around trusting yourself and your own intuition. Mookaite says, "trust yourself."

USE A MOOKIATE PENDULUM FOR:

* decision-making
* gender exploration, gender affirmation
* all readings, personal or for others

PICTURE JASPER

Nature / release / comforting / healing
Root chakra / Capricorn, Scorpio

Picture jasper is said to be a messenger from the Earth Mother, containing information from the past. It gets its name from its complex patterns that almost look like miniature landscape paintings. Picture jasper brings hidden feelings to the surface and releases repression. It is also a useful stone for connecting to past lives and distant realities. Through all of this, picture jasper brings comfort and gently alleviates fear. As a pendulum, picture jasper allows the user to peel back layers of information, like an archeologist carefully brushing away layers of dirt, slowly and gently revealing hidden knowledge and information. Because of its close relationship to the Earth, picture jasper could be a wonderful tool for dowsing, as well as aiding in healing the body and connecting with past lives. Picture jasper is a little piece of Mother Earth.

USE A PICTURE JASPER PENDULUM FOR:

* accessing information
* connecting with past lives
* dowsing
* healing

AVENTURINE

Good luck / manifesting / healing
Heart chakra / Libra / Mercury

Aventurine is *the* good luck crystal. Being a good luck stone, it can help bring things to you, but can also help you focus your wishes and intentions, aiding in manifestation.

Aventurine protects against electromagnetic and environmental pollutants, as well as emanations from cell phones and computers. If you didn't want to use a pendulum made from aventurine, it is a good ally to add into the mix when doing a pendulum reading. It never hurts to have a teammate that can heal and hold space for love and forgiveness, while also lessening the noise from environmental factors like electronics and radio waves. Aventurine cuts through electronic noise.

USE AN ADVENTURING PENDULUM FOR:

* making decisions
* focusing energy

CARNELIAN

Motivation / vitality / energizing / clarity / focus
Sacral, solar plexus chakras / Leo / Sun

Fiery crystals like carnelian might not be the best for everyone because of their almost unmatched intensity. That being said, no one should be afraid or nervous to work with carnelian or other fiery stones, because sometimes what you really need is intense motivation and the driven passion that is a stone ruled by Leo. High energy! Vitality! Motivation! Just like Leos, carnelian is a passionately supportive friend who wants you to realize your own potential. Carnelian is actually very soothing, like sitting by a warm fire (as opposed to something you're going to get burned by). Carnelian is especially skilled at soothing fear and discomfort around death, and can help spirits who have passed. Carnelian is also capable of cleansing spaces, and other crystals.

Carnelian focuses the mind, offers clarity, and aids in concentration. It is especially helpful for ADHD individuals. You would think that such a fiery crystal would overstimulate, but in the same way that stimulants are used to medicate ADHD, like attracts like, and like also soothes like. Fire crystals like carnelian can be like that, so while they may be overwhelming and overstimulating for calmer individuals and people who are neurotypical, they may be just the thing for the neuro-spicy individual (like yours truly). If this describes you, carnelian may become a favorite stone.

USE A CARNELIAN PENDULUM FOR:

* communicating with spirits
* meditation
* cleansing, clearing

KYANITE

Kyanite is a wonderful tool for highly sensitive individuals who are seriously pursuing their spiritual path, or who are beginning this path. Kyanite is a wonderful stone to have in your toolkit. Both blue and black kyanite are intense transmitters and amplifiers of energy and frequencies and stimulate one's psychic abilities and intuition.

BLUE KYANITE

Psychic abilities / intuition / spirits / communication / confidence
Throat chakra / Pisces, Libra / Venus, Moon

Blue kyanite stimulates psychic abilities and intuition while also acting as a kind of antennae for higher vibrations and frequencies. It allows connection to guides and spirits. Blue kyanite also strengthens the voice, encouraging clear communication, while also offering clarity, wisdom, and confidence. It is a wonderful stone if you are channeling or reading for someone, either as a pendulum or presence in your spiritual space.

USE A BLUE KYANITE PENDULUM FOR:

* channeling beings from spiritual realms
* receiving strong messages
* client readings

BLACK KYANITE

Cleansing / protection / unblocking / clarity
Root chakra / Capricorn, Virgo, Scorpio / Saturn, Pluto

Black kyanite is best suited to clearing one's body, auric field, and/or physical space. It's possible to use black kyanite like a brush over the body, shaking away any energy that might be clinging to it. Black kyanite grounds the body and clears negativity and unwanted energy. It removes blockages and illusions, and dispels confusion, allowing space for clear thought. Black kyanite is protective, reassuring, and understanding.

Even if you don't choose a black kyanite pendulum, I recommend that everyone have black kyanite in their arsenal. Plus, its nickname is "witches' broom," so what's not to love?

USE A BLACK KYANITE PENDULUM FOR:

* clearing spaces and energetic bodies
* receiving gentle but needed truths
* healing

MALACHITE

Transformation / honesty / empathy / clarity
Heart chakra / Aquarius / Venus

Malachite is an intense and powerful energetic conduit. It is a strong scrying stone, and can assist in receiving insights from the subconscious, and perhaps messages from the future. Malachite can cut through and clear electromagnetic smog.

When polished and dry, malachite is safe to handle and use. Its toxicity only really rears its head when one is grinding or cutting the stone, so for day-to-day use you are going to be safe. Don't use malachite in a bath or to make a direct contact gem essence (where you put the stone into water to access and utilize its vibrational magic), and be wary of malachite dust if you have a raw crystal. But let's be real: if it was *that* toxic and dangerous, New Age stores wouldn't be selling it in open bins.

Malachite accesses other worlds, both inner and outer, aiding in personal transformation, while also offering space for others' transformation by encouraging honesty and empathy. This is another good crystal for gender exploration and transitions. Malachite opens the heart space.

Malachite is a powerful stone, and you should take time to attune with malachite before using it. Get to know it and connect with it before doing anything too intense. Because of its power, a malachite pendulum holds a lot of potential to be a great boon to the more seasoned pendulum reader or psychic.

USE A MALACHITE PENDULUM FOR:

* channeling messages from other realms
* clearing and cleansing spaces and auric fields
* gender exploration, gender affirmation
* all readings

ROSE QUARTZ

Unconditional love / love in its purest form / healing / calming
Heart chakra / Libra, Taurus, Cancer / Venus

Rose quartz invites in unconditional love and encourages self-forgiveness, self-acceptance, self-trust, and a sense of self-worth. Rose quartz is the true essence of love, and, in many ways, it's the love crystal to end all love crystals. It opens the heart to all levels of inner healing and self-love. It is calming, reassuring, and aids in times of trauma or grief. It can be a bit intense with the big heart feels it helps facilitate, so pairing it with amethyst, garnet, or black tourmaline can help regulate the energy and balance it out.

Rose quartz would make a good pendulum for anyone interested in deepening their self-care and self-compassion. It would be a lovely tool for healing and refocusing energy. Rose quartz is a powerful healer, proficient at taking difficult or uncomfortable emotions and transmuting them into gentler and more positive vibes. This process is never about completely removing difficult energies, but rather shifting them a bit so that healing can be done and peace can come in. Rose quartz rejuvenates, harmonizes, and encourages love in all its forms: platonic love, self-love, communal love, romantic love. Rose quartz has all of the bases covered.

USE A ROSE QUARTZ PENDULUM FOR:

* channeling loving and supportive messages
* heart healing
* transmuting the energy in a space

SELENITE

Cleansing / elevating / intuition / psychic abilities / past lives / subconscious
Crown chakra / Pisces, Cancer / Moon

Selenite is perhaps the most lunar crystal. It carries powerful lunar energy, almost holding the light of the Moon in itself. Selenite cleanses, charges, elevates, and heightens intuition and psychic abilities. Due to its very fine and soft vibration, selenite can neutralize and calm energies. You can use selenite to cleanse anything, from other crystals to an energetic body or space. Selenite can help expand consciousness and connect with higher beings and other realms. It's especially proficient at connecting with lunar deities and angels. Selenite can aid in your navigation and understanding of past lives, and it is also a good guide for offering direction in your current life.

Selenite creates a safe and quiet space that does not allow outside influences in, including anything that might influence the mind. It helps you understand your subconscious by making sense of anything that is coming from your subconscious self. Considering all of its many talents, selenite is a really good choice for a pendulum.

USE A SELENITE PENDULUM FOR:

* cleansing or clearing
* physical healing
* communicating with angels

* receiving guidance and support
* deciphering messages that come from your subconscious

MOONSTONE

Fresh start / awareness / psychic abilities / clairvoyance
Crown chakra / Pisces, Cancer / Moon

Moonstone is a lunar crystal that is intuitive, reflective, and reminds you that everything is part of a cycle. It aligns in particular with the New Moon, acting as "a stone of new beginnings." Moonstone reminds us to go with the flow and not get hung up on details. It connects with the subconscious, bringing that experience forward to the conscious self. Moonstone would make a wonderful pendulum for any practitioner because it really speaks to the subconscious, and already works to interpret these messages. Moonstone heightens psychic abilities, develops clairvoyance, and encourages you to not only accept but also *trust* your psychic gifts.

USE A MOONSTONE PENDULUM FOR:

* planning and organizing
* connecting with your subconscious self
* all readings, especially if you're new to receiving messages for yourself or others

HOWLITE

Calming / wisdom / insight / focus / clarity
Crown, third eye chakras / Aquarius, Libra / Venus, Pluto

Howlite is a very calming stone, and a wonderful ally for anyone who may be struggling with insomnia, anxiety, or any difficulties presented by an overactive mind. This stone can link into spiritual realms and dimensions and opens up the individual to receive wisdom and insight. Focusing on a piece of howlite is said to transport you to another time or dimension. Howlite's ability to still the mind and transmute difficult emotions (especially stress or anger) makes it a valuable stone for meditation and for doing readings. As a pendulum, howlite is wonderful at discerning useful information and cutting away any doubt or fear around receiving messages. Howlite expands the consciousness, opening you up to receiving what you need to hear and letting go of anything false or untrue. Howlite recognizes honesty and truth.

USE A HOWLITE PENDULUM FOR:

* clearing the energetic self
* meditation before bed
* all readings

ONYX

Grounding / stabilizing / protection / divination / confidence
Root chakra / Capricorn, Scorpio / Saturn, Pluto

Onyx is deeply grounding, stabilizing, and protective. When polished, onyx would be a marvelous scrying surface. Being a scrying stone, onyx is already well suited to being used in different forms of divination. Onyx is supportive, helping you build self-confidence and protecting against fear. In ancient Rome, onyx amulets were carried into battle to promote courage. Onyx creates a barrier against unwanted and unneeded energies. It is also a very practical stone, encouraging practicality and preparedness. Supportive onyx helps you listen to your own advice, and helps recognize and integrate dualities within the self.

Onyx could be a comfort to a nonbinary person, as it helps remove discomfort and stress around dichotomies, and allows the individual to just exist as a whole and complete person, while also celebrating nonbinary energy. It is uniting, while also being complementary and stabilizing.

As a pendulum, onyx can be tricky to navigate. It is said to hold the memories of things that have happened to the wearer or the holder. This could be really valuable to a medium who channels through psychometry and physical contact. (Psychometry is a form of ESP characterized by the ability to glean information by making physical contact with an object; it is a type of scrying in which the intuitive or psychic trigger is the object.) A piece of onyx could allow access to a great deal of information, depending on who has handled it or where it's been. The flip side is, if you are the owner of an onyx pendulum and you are using it to get information on someone else, you might find that you'll start getting a lot of crossed wires and maybe even some confusion in the reading. Onyx is also very secretive and connected to its holder, so while it's easy to attune to and connect with, it may not be the best tool to use when reading for someone else. But if someone were to read you, using your pendulum as a trigger could unlock some deep information about you (*if* onyx decides to reveal that information).

Onyx is very supportive, healing, and transformative. It's perhaps not the best choice as a pendulum, at least not for a novice reader, but it is a valuable crystal familiar—an entity that helps you in your magic—that is easy to bond with. In fact, if you acquired a piece of onyx carved to look like your animal familiar, onyx would be a next-level protector, secret-keeper, and friend.

USE AN ONYX PENDULUM FOR:

* personal readings and self-work
* developing your own craft and practice
* connecting with your subconscious and inner secrets

CRYSTAL QUARTZ (*also known as clear quartz*)

Master healer / amplifier / multipurpose
All chakras, but especially crown / all signs / Sun, Moon

Crystal quartz is the master healer, holding the ability to do it all. Quartz amplifies energy, and also has the ability to absorb, store, release, regulate, and unblock. To say that quartz is the most essential stone to have in one's arsenal feels hyperbolic, but it's almost an understatement. Crystals with more specific purposes are wonderful, but you can't beat the all-purpose magic of crystal quartz. And when you pair it with something else? **chef's kiss** Quartz has the ability to attune to your specific spiritual purpose, and it can harmonize energies. If you have a specific need but you can't access other crystals, you can take a moment to charge or program crystal quartz to your specifications to meet that need. It's easily cleansed and charged, and a small piece goes a long way. You don't need much crystal quartz to be effective. It's truly a team player.

USE A QUARTZ PENDULUM FOR:

* all readings
* clearing, cleansing
* charging other stones or tools

SODALITE

Intuition / communication / confidence / creativity
Throat chakra / Sagittarius / Neptune

Sodalite opens up spiritual awareness and brings the higher mind down to the physical, uniting the logical and the intuitive. Sodalite would be a wonderful choice for a pendulum, encouraging communication, confidence, flow, serenity, and intellectual stimulation. This stone calms the mind and eliminates distraction, as well as clears electromagnetic pollution. Sodalite would also be beneficial for anyone aiming to use a pendulum for more creative pursuits, as it enhances creativity and focus. It encourages honesty as well as positive self-expression, induces deep meditative states, and aids in the search for truth. Sodalite also clears away dogmatic and blinkered thinking, allowing the holder to open up to more intuitive understanding and objectivity.

Sodalite encourages radical honesty and openness, allowing one to circumvent uncertainty, dogma, and dichotomous thinking. As a pendulum, sodalite encourages free communication between the conscious and unconscious minds, as well as more direct communication with others, corporeal or not. It's a fine stone for creative and intuitive individuals who struggle with trusting their gifts and abilities.

USE A SODALITE PENDULUM FOR:

* creative pursuits
* gathering inspiration
* meditation
* receiving detailed messages

LABRADORITE (*also known as spectrolite*)

Healing / protection / support / encouragement
Crown, throat chakras / Scorpio, Dark Moon Pisces / Saturn, Pluto, Chiron

Labradorite is mystical and protective, a stone that raises consciousness and connects with the energies of the universe. It also prevents energy leakage, allowing you to keep your energy, rather than it being lost to others. Labradorite, with its flash of color and mysterious shine, aligns the physical and the energetic bodies. It stimulates intuition and heightens psychic abilities, all the while allowing you to shed illusions and cut through to the absolute truth of the matter.

Labradorite is a supportive companion, devoted to encouraging your best strengths while also protecting you. It is transformative, and a strong ally for when you are navigating big changes in your life, especially surrounding spiritual transformation, magical growth, and grief. It encourages mental clarity and positive communication, allowing you to be honest with everyone, and especially with yourself.

USE A LABRADORITE PENDULUM FOR:

* introspective readings
* guidance
* receiving supportive messages

BLACK TOURMALINE (*also known as schorl*)

Protection / grounding / psychic armor / objective neutrality
All chakras / Capricorn / Earth

BIG PROTECTION ENERGY. Black tourmaline is almost overly intense in its ability to protect. Black tourmaline is like a weighted blanket, a castle wall made of granite and steel, an impenetrable suit of armor. It's chainmail for the spiritual self. It draws off negativity and unwanted energies, offering stability and balance in their wake. This stone can be too heavy (spiritually) for some, but if you ever have issues with grounding or calling back your energy, you can't ask for a better crystal daddy than black tourmaline. Along with being spiritually protective, black tourmaline protects against electronic smog and radiation, making it a good stone to keep near devices and electronics. I keep a huge piece on my desk, and another smaller, but equally powerful, piece near my gaming consoles. I also tend to have a piece somewhere on my person. Black tourmaline may well be my favorite stone because of how grounding it is (I have a lot of fire placements, so I need a lot of grounding).

It's also a stone that protects against spells, psychic attacks, and ill wishes. It allows objective neutrality. Black tourmaline helps you draw from your own inner strengths and vitality without completely depleting yourself. As a pendulum, black tourmaline would be a good choice for someone who has a tendency to pick up on *all of the energies* around them. Black tourmaline amplifies this ability, while also protecting the individual from harm. Black tourmaline creates a greater awareness of all things.

USE A BLACK TOURMALINE PENDULUM FOR:

* clearing and cleansing
* introspection and personal messages
* all readings

SERPENTINE

Divine feminine / healing / calming / stabilizing
Heart, crown chakras / Gemini / Venus, Saturn

A very Venusian stone in shadowy and mysterious ways (coming from the Saturnian influences), serpentine promotes gradual healing, softly and intentionally. It promotes feelings of peace and calm, and stabilizes the mind. Serpentine is a strong tool for meditation, and is good at memory retrieval, helping you gain wisdom and activate psychic gifts. It is also a good stone for soothing anxious minds and anxious hearts.

Serpentine opens up new pathways for Kundalini (coiled snake, a form of divine feminine energy located at the base of the spine), and is a strong stone for devotional practices around Hekate and other serpent deities.

Serpentine is grounding, without closing off your crown or third eye chakras.

USE A SERPENTINE PENDULUM FOR:

* healing
* meditation
* accessing past-life information
* all readings

SUNSTONE

Inspiration / supportive / boundaries / joy / transmutative / optimism
Sacral chakra, solar plexus / Leo / Sun

Sunstone is joyful, buoyant, and inspiring. It is a very encouraging stone, which, like a Leo friend, is always there to support you in being your best self. Sunstone encourages the holder to say NO and set boundaries. It helps you call back your energy, and also removes energetic "hooks" from other people (and vice versa). This stone can act as an antidepressant, pulling you out of dark pits and feelings of despair while increasing self-worth and confidence. Sunstone can also help transmute heavy or difficult emotions, making space for optimism and lighter feelings. At the very least, it will ease difficult feelings and make them easier to carry.

Sunstone makes for a pendulum that aids in the flow of creative ideas, as well as the transmission of positive messages that one may not be open to hearing otherwise. Sunstone is reliable, generous, and full of vitality and compassionate energy. Sunstone wouldn't be the best choice if reading for other people, but it is a stable and beneficial ally for self-work and introspection, as it allows the true self to shine through.

Sunstone is also a "get up and go" stone, so you may find yourself wanting to move your body a bit after working with sunstone.

USE A SUNSTONE PENDULUM FOR:

* receiving joyful and supportive messages
* creativity and inspiration
* introspection and personal work

TIGER'S EYE

Stability / grounding / clarity / focus / awareness
Root chakra / Capricorn, Taurus, Leo, Virgo / Earth, Sun

Tiger's eye is a multifaceted stone (pardon the pun?) that harnesses the fierceness and fiery energy of the Sun, with the stability and grounding of Earth. Tiger's eye reminds us that we are a part of the Earth, not apart from it (paraphrased from Marie Williams Cornelio, a color and gemstone practitioner who channeled the contents of her book *Gemstones and Color (and a Whole Lot More)* from Marjorie Buckley Turcotte).

Tiger's eye (as well as the similar stone, cat's eye) enables you to "see in the dark" (like its feline namesake), allowing the holder to dispel illusions, recognize the truth, and focus on what's really important. Tiger's eye conjures grounding energy that also makes space for enlightenment. Tiger's eye crystals vary greatly from stone to stone, just like the feline energies that follow them. Tiger's eye is another stone that is deeply personal, allowing an opportunity for deep connection and a powerful relationship between you and the stone. As such, it's not really something to use in relation to others, unless the stone is cleansed regularly after every person. Tiger's eye can be given as a gift, but ensure full and complete cleansing before giving it to the intended. As a pendulum, tiger's eye is a wonderful choice for self-work and introspection. It really does aid in clarity, making it a strong ally for recognizing truths. It is also helpful in receiving and relaying important messages. Tiger's eye enhances psychic abilities and practical perception. When tiger's eye has a message for you, you listen. Think of it as a familiar gently guiding you to what you need, persistent until the message is received, acknowledged, and understood.

USE A TIGER'S EYE PENDULUM FOR:

* introspection
* personal guidance
* connecting with guides and familiars
* receiving honest messages

Witch Tip

Having a million pendulums with different uses and purposes can get expensive and can become difficult to keep organized. Instead of having a different crystal pendulum for different purposes (e.g., quartz for healing, black tourmaline for clearing, sodalite for spirit communication, howlite for meditation), consider getting an empty cage pendulum. This is a metal pendulum with a top that opens and closes with a small latch. They are often decorated with Celtic knots or pentacles. It can hold any small crystal of your choice, allowing you to interchange the crystal with what you need at that moment, or a couple of different crystals that will play together nicely for your current goal. Plus, now any crystals you might use here for a pendulum session can be cleansed and used for other purposes!

I started doing this, using a small piece of amethyst in my cage pendulum. I'm very pleased with the results I've been getting!

Other Materials

Nature is malleable, offering so many materials that we can use. We have the ability to pull things from the Earth that require little manipulation to make them workable. These kinds of materials have been used by humans for millennia, and extend beyond the wood, stone, and metals described earlier. The materials I'm including in this section have been used for making art, tools, and more by our ancient ancestors as well as modern-day people. I will touch on other man-made materials in Chapter 8.

CERAMICS

Protection / creation / humanity / bonding / ancestral connection
All chakras / All zodiac signs / Earth

Ceramic pendulums have a close connection to the Earth from whence they come, with the added energy of the individual who crafted them. Ceramics is one of the most universally human mediums. Archeologists have found ceramics around the world, with ceramic artifacts dating back to at least 24,000 BCE. Ceramic items are human: they are made for practical use, as well as for aesthetics and art for art's sake. It's a material that is not advisable to use in weaponry because of how brittle it can be, but it has been used in body armor, and ceramic blades do exist. However, it is true that it is fragile. Anything created from clay is beautiful but can be easily destroyed, symbolizing an acceptance that not everything can last forever.

A pendulum made of clay will have a tendency to warm itself to an individual. Materials that inspire both beauty and utilitarian practicality are a good choice for magic, because by their nature they are easy to bond with, especially if the ceramic is crafted by an individual maker. Ceramic items hold on to the energy of memory. For this reason, I would recommend cleansing any secondhand ceramics that you are bringing into your home. It's very fortunate that handwashing for sanitary purposes doubles, in this case, as metaphysical and energetic cleansing.

A pendulum crafted by the hands of an artisan for an individual would be a deeply intimate tool, acting as an ally that can understand and hold space for the holder. A ceramic is both incredibly old and newly birthed, so as a material it can be thorough and expansive in the information and energy it presents to the individual. Ceramic items have ancient wisdom, but are also able to look at things from a fresh perspective. Expect a ceramic tool (magical or mundane) to be able to perceive multiple points of view.

A ceramic's ability to discern multiple perspectives means that if you're using a ceramic pendulum, you should be very clear and precise in the questions you ask. It might be helpful to use a pendulum board or chart with a ceramic pendulum (we'll discuss this later on).

BONE/IVORY/ANIMAL PARTS

Correspondences vary depending on the animal and the origin, but all are ruled by the Earth, Sun, and Moon (to varying degree)

A quick note on ivory (included in this section because it does exist, and it does come from animals) and ethics. The purchase and sale of ivory is illegal and unethical. Still, it was relatively common for a long time, and because of this, someone's grandparent or another family member may have left them some ivory, or perhaps they found some at a misinformed (or under-informed) antique or vintage store.

There are any number of scenarios in which an individual may acquire something like ivory. It raises the question of what someone would do with such a thing. Not even just ivory, but other materials or artifacts that may have been acquired though illegal or unethical means. Do we destroy them? Do we return them to the place from whence they came? Do we continue to use them, while doing our best to honor the origins of the material? I don't think that there's an easy answer. I raise this point because the ethics of certain materials within magical and metaphysical communities is constantly up for debate, with many individuals and businesses skirting the line of what is and isn't ethical, with varying levels of transparency around where an item is obtained, who can or cannot utilize tools, and practices that may be closed or limited.

I encourage all interested in—or actively involved in—magical practices to decolonize their craft and be as ethical as possible. What's nice about being ethical in the realm of magic is that it actually makes the craft more accessible, both in terms of practicality and expenses. It means purchasing more items secondhand, or sourcing materials and tools within one's own community. Ethical witchcraft can mean a lot of things, but a big part of it for me is being aware of my surroundings and the land on which I live. Not only being aware of what plants live in and around my home, but also knowing and understanding the indigenous land that I am living on. Knowing ancestral names for the rivers and the mountains around me. Being aware of my impact, not only to other humans, but also to the animals and plants that live around me.

One could use a piece of bone or another animal part as a pendulum. In my own practice, I avoid the use of animal products, unless I know exactly where they come from. This usually means that I find something, usually bone, on a walk or while doing other magic. I don't take anything unless I have clear consent or instruction to do so. I can trust that some people craft with ethically sourced bones or animal material, just by nature of who they are, but I am skeptical (at best) about the animal parts that are sold in some witchcraft or occult shops. It's largely a numbers game. Realistically, if a shop has dozens of pieces of taxidermy of the same animal (looking at you, people who decorate dead ducks in silly costumes) or there are dozens of the same type of claws from an animal . . . maybe it's a little unlikely that those animals' bodies were acquired ethically. Maybe it's more likely that their present remains are a by-product of something a bit more unsavory that most people don't want to think about. To bring that type of energy into your space, into your magic . . . personally, that's not something I want to take a gamble on.

Like the secondhand or heirloom ivory, it's ultimately up to the individual to decide what feels most comfortable. Some people are okay with looking past (or actively ignoring) the harsh reality of what goes into certain parts of our lives, or what goes on in the world around us every day. There's also the point of capacity that all of us have when considering ethics or morals. It can be easy to spring into action when something is happening right in front of us, but it is exhausting to consider realities beyond what is in front of us right now. We all have the responsibility to make decisions for ourselves, but it is not our responsibility to police others for their choices or how they live their lives. We are, by and large, just doing our best. Everything is nuanced, and nothing is black and white.

So, what about using any animal parts as a pendulum, or crafting a pendulum from a preexisting animal bone or tooth or claw? Yes, you can do it. Using an animal's body part in magic will connect your divination or your magic or your spell to the spirit of that particular animal, as well as the general egregore version of that animal. (An egregore is a spirit or entity that is a result of collective thought and imagination, kind of a manifestation of a

Quick Notes on Foraging or Finding

Just because you can take something doesn't mean that it's yours. Just because something is available, doesn't mean it's yours. Learn to connect with the energy of plants and nonliving allies in your surroundings. Learn to ask for permission before cutting or taking. Some beings in the outside world are entirely enthusiastic, but others would really rather be left alone. Not everything wants to be involved with humans. A helpful tool can be visualizing that everything has body language. Look at that beautiful flower, and imagine that it can communicate through its body, like a wild animal. What is this flower, this wild being, saying to you? Is it sniffing your hand, or is it snarling and running away? Learning to communicate with plants and other nonhuman beings on a whole can help you in many ways, including honing your intuition and deepening your connection with the wild world. Practices like this will deepen your understanding of your place in the world and the power you hold as a human. Ethical magic is recognizing that power, but not exploiting it. Ethical magic is recognizing that everything functions in balance, and we have a responsibility to be stewards of that balance.

being created by many people. It is an entity that is brought into being by collective manifestation and thought forming.) So, it's not really the spirit of just one animal, but the spiritual essence of an animal, created through the collective understanding of what that animal is. An essence created through symbols, mythology, folklore, biology, and individual experiences. Some of the pieces that contribute to this spirit's identity might not be seen or felt, but they are present like DNA. The way someone experiences this spirit, this animal being, will be completely unique to them, informed by personal understanding and experience, and their own cultural background. If someone from North America were to use a fox tooth as their pendulum, their experience would be different from someone in Japan using a similar tool. Even within North America, the experiences would be incredibly varied. An indigenous individual may have a different understanding of the animal than someone who is a settler or immigrant. Our experiences are always informed by our individual histories, and with something like an animal, there is so much variety in how we interact and exist with it. Yet, there are always universal truths, and overlap in those understandings.

When they're alive, animals have lives and personalities that we don't usually see (unless the animal is a pet, a farm animal, or otherwise domesticated or in captivity), but different species do have characteristics and traits that become associated with them. These traits, too, lend themselves to these spiritual essences.

When the animal dies, or is killed, its essence remains attached to its body. The same is true for humans and pets, but we have trouble feeling that essence because the being we were familiar with is gone, their body feeling and looking incredibly changed, and somehow distinctly unwhole. We can only really feel the absence, so the ability to feel any kind of essence or remaining energy is incredibly difficult, and not something most people would want to do. With animals and even human remains from individuals we didn't know personally, it can be easier to feel that essence. The energetic imprint of life stays on everything that was once living, just as any nonliving being carries their own energy. Energy persists in every part of the world. Working with anything that was once fully alive can be difficult for some, because the energetic imprint may be too much. Conversely, someone who wishes to work deeply with death and the underworld may find this type of energy to be useful, and maybe even comfortable.

To use an animal part as a pendulum, or to use a pendulum made from animal remains, you could approach it in one of two ways (or even a combination of the two):

* Use the pendulum as a means to connect with that particular animal or essence, to get answers directly from them. This may create a relationship similar to having a familiar, so getting to know the spirit would be essential to the process. Careful selection would be encouraged, as some may not be interested in being involved in divination or witchcraft in this way. Not every animal is interested in, or means to be, a familiar. It's personal and varied. One consideration may be to work with an animal you cared for, and one who was already your familiar. It's morbid, but one could place ashes from their beloved animal into a small vial or pendant, and use that as the weight for a pendulum. This would allow you to continue working with your familiar in a meaningful way (if they're interested).

* Use the pendulum as a means to divine through and with the essence and presence of death. This would technically be necromancy, which always sounds far more intense than it actually is (necromancy is divination with the help of the dead, not re-animating skeletons and corpses). This kind of approach probably wouldn't be for everyone, which is okay. Death magic and witchcraft that focuses on death can be a bit too sinister for some (maybe most).

Ultimately, I don't know if I would recommend using animal remains (human included) in any divinatory practices, at least so far as using the remains as a tool like a pendulum. That amount of energy can be volatile, so it can take something that is relatively straightforward (like a pendulum reading) and turn it into something that not only requires more energy, but may be difficult to interpret and understand. Anything in the aether or existing on different planes (spirits and entities) is unlikely to be straight up dishonest, but they can be cryptic, misleading, and have the potential to be somewhat deceptive. If an individual did wish to go down this path, I would encourage them to use the pendulum in conjunction with a pendulum board, as well as any tools that can help them channel more completely and provide clearer images, such as a tarot deck or scrying mirror.

Chapter 7

PENDULUM SHAPES AND TYPES

If a shape can be suspended from a line, it can be used as or made into a pendulum. There are shapes that are more common than others, and some pendulums were specifically "created" for radiesthesia—they actually were invented for the purpose. Others were appropriated, including the shape of wadj amulets. The wadj-style pendulum is typically called the Thoth pendulum, and it is one of the many pendulums popularized by radiesthesists that are still used, and readily available in occult shops, today.

When it comes to crystal pendulums, some schools of thought suggest that certain shapes are best suited to certain tasks (for example, a hexagonal pendulum with a point is better for focusing and directing energy). I think that this is a bit untrue. Yes, a crystal in its rawest state will be more powerful, with a higher vibration (and sometimes it can be too intense for some individuals), but let's be real and practical: a rock, when cut and polished, is still that rock. The chemical compounds and geological structures remain unchanged. The rock is changed, but no more than if you were to get a piercing, a tattoo, or just a haircut. These modifications to your outward appearance might change how you feel, but the core of who you are is unchanged. I don't think that crystals are any different; they're smarter than us, and they know who and what they are. Outward appearance has little, if anything, to do with the true essence of an individual. Outward appearance does not indicate value or ability. The correspondences and uses of the stone are more important than its appearance, in terms of whether it is cut, polished, tumbled, carved, or drilled. If a crystal is well suited to a pendulum, it will be so regardless of its shape. However, intention does matter, and if the shape of a pendulum is created or selected with intention, it will play into the effectiveness of the pendulum itself. Shapes have their own powers and correspondences, and you can use those to your advantage.

The one benefit that certain shapes may have, depending on what you're using the pendulum for, is that some may be easier to read when using the pendulum in conjunction with a pendulum board or chart. A pendulum with a point may be easier to interpret and read. But if you're using a pendulum without a board, either for divination or healing, the shape likely won't matter. Personally, that's why I like having a few pendulums kicking around, or the option to make one. Just as I keep different tarot decks for different purposes (for example, the cards I use for readings for others, as opposed to the cards I use for personal readings), having options can be beneficial depending on the day and the intention for the reading.

BASIC SHAPES

To begin, let's look at the building blocks of all shapes, two-dimensional and three-dimensional alike. From these basics, we can better evaluate what certain shapes would be best used for, as pendulums or otherwise in magical practices. From the three basic shapes, we can even create formulas or cheat sheets for what certain shapes would be good for.

Circle

A circle pendulum is a simple closed polygon with either zero, one, or infinite sides. If a straight line on a polygon is a side, a circle would have zero, but one might argue that a circle has, in fact, infinite sides—which feels very metaphysical. A circle being simultaneously nothing and everything is a fascinating concept, and it does hint at how it could be used in a magical sense. Because of its lack of, or infinite, sides, a circle radiates energy in all directions. A circle encloses, protects. In magic, circles seal spells and create magical barriers. Many traditions have the practitioner cast a circle before doing any spellwork. Circles are endless, unobstructed. Circles facilitate movement.

In theory, because the circle causes energy to radiate outward, a circle or sphere crystal wouldn't need to be cleansed or charged, because the shape allows it to cycle through and recycle energy. The energy is in perpetual motion, making it suitable for healing and clearing.

RELATED SHAPES INCLUDE:

* cylinder
* sphere
* amorphous (shapeless, but lack of sides makes it closer to circle than not)
* oval
* egg shape

Rectangle or Square

A rectangular or square pendulum consists of a polygon with four sides, meeting at 90-degree angles. A rectangle, as well as related shapes like a square (a rectangle with four equal sides), often represents structure, tradition, rigidity, foundation, and logic. The square as a shape would correspond closely to the tarot card The Emperor, whereas the circle would be more like The Empress. The square, The Emperor, represents creation through building, structure, and foundation. The circle, The Empress, represents creation through wholeness, infinity, nature, and natural formation.

These shapes allow formation and construction. Patterns are recognized and discerned. Structures created by rectangular shapes carry rigidity and lack flexibility. Squares and four-sided polygons like them don't generally make appearances in magic, aside from sometimes representing the four earthly elements. Squares don't lend themselves to a lot of magical practices, but they do make themselves known in the practical and the mundane by way of books and tarot cards. A rectangular shape could be used in a pendulum, but it would be more suited as a combination with triangular elements to facilitate the movement of energy.

RELATED SHAPES INCLUDE:

* square
* rectangle
* cube
* hexagon
* tetragon
* triclinic
* monoclinic
* an argument could be made that a cylinder combines circular and rectangular qualities

Triangle

A triangular pendulum is a three-sided polygon, with the sides meeting at different angles. The triangle is always a triangle, but the length of sides and degree of angles can further define the shape. An equilateral triangle (one with equal-length sides, and three internal degrees of 60 degrees each, for a total of 180) is a shape with a lot of structural integrity, offering a strong foundation. Triangles can represent balance, direction, and movement, and are also visual representations of anything to do with the number 3. In the realm of the magical, the triangle manifests in a lot of commonplace pendulums, as well as the witch's hat (sometimes considered a cone of power).

RELATED SHAPES INCLUDE:

* cone
* trigonal
* orthorhombic

From the basic shapes, we can get a general idea of what other shapes would be good for. Think of it as a math problem. (Sorry to all of the math-dislikers. Bear with me for a minute.)

For example, if a circle = healing, and a square = practicality, then a combination of the two would be a good source of healing that is down to earth and grounding.

Circle Keywords

* infinite energy
* wholeness
* healing
* completeness
* all directions
* perpetual energy
* infinity

Square/Rectangle Keywords

* structure
* foundation
* logic
* practicality
* information
* messages
* grounded

Triangle Keywords

* direction
* balance
* movement
* foundation
* mystical

Cone = Triangle + Circle

* directed healing
* powerful, focused energy
* allows the flow of energy

Natural Points = Square + Triangle

* affirmative grounded energy
* flow of supportive energy
* smooth transmission of information

Pyramid = Square + Triangle

* transmission of information
* directed messages
* flow of intuition

A diamond shape could be considered a square, or it could be viewed as two triangles, depending on the intention.

TYPES OF PENDULUMS

Some pendulums have been created by or popularized by different dowsers and radiesthesists. Many pendulums are named after Egyptian gods, due to the time and place in which they were conceptualized. Each pendulum has different abilities and uses, but if you found any of these pendulums out in the wild (so to speak) and they connected with you, you could use them for any pendulum work that you choose.

Universal Pendulum

This spherical pendulum was developed in France in 1936 by dowsers Leon Chaumery, Andre de Belizal, and Paul-Andre Morel. The Universal Pendulum (U.P.) is used predominantly in diagnosing and healing through color codes and color therapy. It is also useful at recognizing and determining environmental stressors.

Isis Pendulum

Named after the Egyptian goddess, the Isis pendulum features a stacked disc design, with those rings acting as amplifiers. This design makes the pendulum very sensitive for dowsing, as well as a strong conduit for receiving information and healing. There are many variations of the Isis pendulum, with different numbers of discs. The more discs, the more sensitive the Isis pendulum, but they are all good for healing and dowsing. The Isis pendulum is always cleansing itself by the way it emits energy.

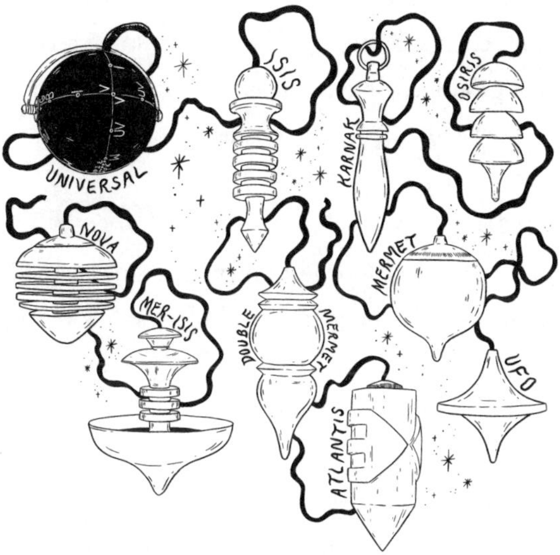

Karnak Pendulum

Based on the shape of ancient Egyptian wadj amulets, the Karnak pendulum is said to be highly sensitive, especially for dowsing metals, minerals, and water. This pendulum is also said to be particularly successful for map dowsing.

Note: The Karnak pendulum is appropriated from ancient Egyptian funerary amulets. As such, I'm reluctant to recommend this particular pendulum.

Osiris Pendulum

The Osiris pendulum's unique shape amplifies its own energy, making it a strong pendulum for research purposes, dowsing, and divination. It can work by "leading" energy away from the subject, so it's recommended that this pendulum be grounded or left in a neutral space when not in use. It's also said to be really powerful, so it's not considered a pendulum for beginners.

Nova Pendulum

This pendulum acts like the Isis pendulum, with a similar ring-like structure. However, the shape is more spherical, making it a soft and gentle pendulum that radiates energy from all angles. The Nova pendulum is rejuvenating, and very good for healing and clearing.

Mermet Pendulum

The Mermet pendulum was developed by Abbe Mermet and is believed to be the first pendulum with a "witness chamber," meaning that the top can be unscrewed to reveal a space that can hold samples. This can be useful, because with dowsing (as with a lot of magic), "like attracts like," so placing a sample of something can help the dowser find specific things. For example, putting oil into this cavity would help find oil, gold would find gold, water would find water, and so on. This space can also hold samples that help you focus on a specific question and get more accurate answers, look for allergens in food, or determine if something is suited to you and your magical practice. The sky's the limit!

The Mermet is sometimes also called a "two-piece" pendulum. This terminology could also be used in relation to the Double Mermet pendulum, discussed next, as well as any pendulum that comes apart into two pieces and has a chamber for samples.

Double Mermet Pendulum

The Double Mermet has a witness chamber like the Mermet pendulum, but the shape of the pendulum makes it more sensitive. Not only is it useful for dowsing, but it is also a valuable tool for divination and finding answers. The pointed shape on the lower half also makes it well suited to doing readings with a pendulum board or chart.

Mer-Isis Pendulum

Combining the shapes of the Isis and Mermet pendulums, this pendulum features the amplifying rings and the large, round base. The Mer-Isis pendulum is one of the best pendulums for healing, chakra balancing, and releasing pain. It's a good pendulum choice for anyone, beginners and experts alike.

Atlantean Pendulum

This pendulum incorporates the same design as the Atlantis Ring, which is said to protect the individual against harm (the pendulum is said to do the same). Useful for healing and therapy, as well as harmonizing and balancing energies, the Atlantean pendulum is a powerful instrument for change as well as self-work.

UFO Pendulum

Named for its shape, the UFO pendulum is a great tool for processing energy. The UFO pendulum was designed by Jozef Baj, a Polish engineer and radiesthesist who studied the works of Chaumery, de Belizal, and Morel, using his research to further develop his own pendulum designs. In fact, many of the pendulums in this section were designed and perfected by Baj.

The UFO pendulum is sensitive to energy and vibrations, making it a valuable tool for dowsing and healing. It is especially well suited to working outside, as its shape allows it to remain relatively unaffected by the elements. The UFO pendulum truly is an MVP that would be a useful tool for any pendulum user.

The Hebrew Pendulum (a.k.a. Metutelet)

The Metutelet (Hebrew for pendulum) is made of a thick cotton string and a wooden cylinder. The rope is knotted on both sides, passing all the way through the cylinder. Because it is knotted at both ends, the pendulum can be used in two ways, depending on which of its two flat surfaces is facing upward. One of those surfaces features a smooth face that is used to diagnose the subject, determining what is going on with the individual receiving a reading or being healed. The opposite face is grooved, and it is used to clear and heal. This variety of pendulum is named for its use of Hebrew words, selected for their high vibrations and energies. The words are written or printed on small pieces of paper, which are then fixed to the cylinder with a rubber band. The letters chosen are meant to help the pendulum focus on the most beneficial energies in order to restore harmony and balance to the subject. This pendulum is predominantly used in radiesthesia, intended to help heal and clear the subject's energy.

Most sources credit Pierre Heli with the popularization of this pendulum, and others point to a connection with the Knights Templar. In reality, the Hebrew pendulum was written about by Jean de la Foye, with the most detailed descriptions and explanations found in his 1975 book *Ondes de Vie, Ondes de Mort* (*Waves of Life, Waves of Death*). Jean de la Foye goes into detail about the Hebrew letters chosen, crediting the research to J. G. Bardet. De la Foye also describes and explains a few different types of pendulums used for radiesthesia.

I'm not sure why Pierre Heli is credited with the Hebrew pendulum. Most places where one could purchase one of these pendulums reference Pierre Heli in the same way, almost verbatim. I dug into Pierre Heli as much as I could for this book, but found nothing. I'm not even convinced that Pierre Heli was a real person. If he was, I couldn't find any writing that he did about dowsing, pendulums, or the occult, and no one else has written about him in any great detail. Once again, the pendulum is mythologized, though saying that almost gives too much credit to such erroneous and confusing fabrications.

OTHER TYPES OF PENDULUMS

These pendulums largely combine shapes of other pendulums, accessing the power of different designs to achieve specific purposes. The more specific the form of the pendulum, the more specialized its use. This list is by no means extensive or conclusive.

* Osiris-Isis
* Seven Archangels
* Soul
* Flower of Life
* Eye of Ra
* Benedictine
* Hathor
* Virtual Cone
* Enel
* Spiral
* Yoni
* Schuessler Salt pendulum sets
* Neutral

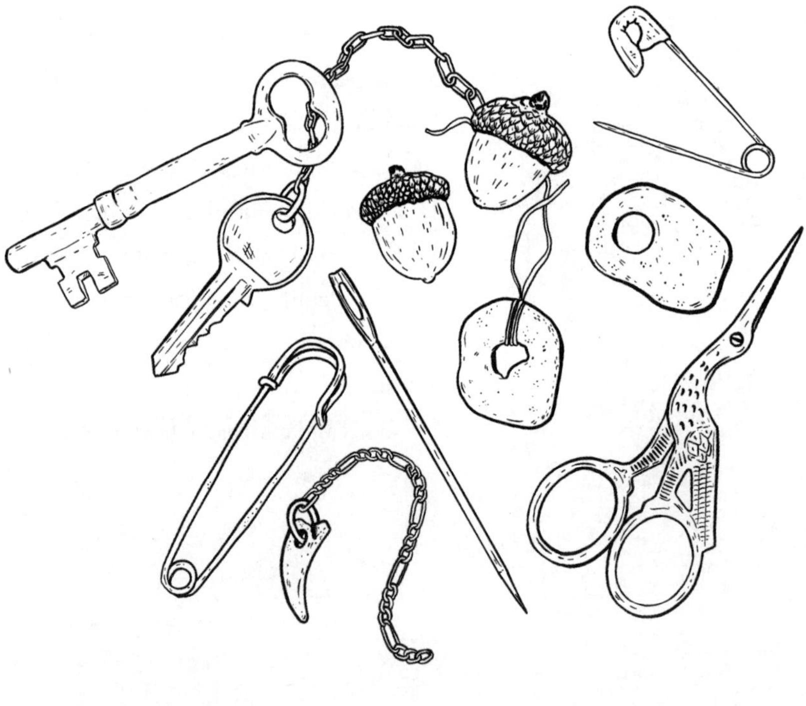

99 Objects That Can Be Used as a Pendulum Once a Thread or Chain Is Added

1. Key
2. Crucifix or cross
3. Hamsa
4. Star of David
5. Any religious symbol
6. Measuring spoon
7. Necklace
8. Earring
9. Charm
10. Acorn, pinecone, hazelnut
11. Ring
12. Knitting needle
13. Sewing needle
14. Hag stone
15. Plumb bob
16. Drop spindle
17. Scissor
18. Wood piece, twig
19. Bolo tie (the heavier the slide, the better)
20. Yo-yo
21. Small toy
22. Metal ornament
23. Button
24. Censer (the incense burner on a chain, commonly used in the Catholic Church)
25. Unlit candle (especially one with an untrimmed wick)
26. Phone charger
27. Ball of wax
28. Pen, pencil
29. Magnet
30. Padlock
31. Eating utensil
32. Corkscrew
33. Screw
34. Nail
35. Bulldog clip
36. Pocket knife
37. Lightbulb
38. Safety pin
39. Kilt pin
40. Clothespin
41. Lace bobbin
42. Thread bobbin
43. Spool of thread
44. Paper clip
45. Eraser
46. Roll of tape
47. Yoni egg
48. Ben Wa ball
49. Bullet vibrator

50. Lip balm
51. Coin
52. Bottle cap
53. Paintbrush, makeup brush
54. Napkin ring
55. Small wrench or screwdriver
56. Dice
57. Keychain
58. Lucky rabbit's foot
59. Wishbone
60. Small bone
61. Tooth
62. Ankh charm
63. Rosary beads
64. Pentagram charm
65. Bookmark made of something other than paper
66. Any token or charm that holds spiritual meaning or value for you
67. Small jar or bottle (you can even find some mini bottles that are meant to be used in jewelry, so they have an eyelet screw and/or a jump ring attached)
68. Evil eye charm
69. Brooch
70. Seashell
71. Miniature book
72. Dollhouse miniature
73. Tabletop role-playing miniature
74. Bell
75. Cat or dog toy
76. Piece of coral
77. Locket
78. Coffin nail
79. Meaningful talisman
80. Dried fruit
81. Phallus amulet
82. Bead
83. Horse harness brass
84. Earbud
85. Clove or bulb of garlic
86. Piece of ginger
87. Razor blade
88. Chess piece
89. Lighter
90. Prescription bottle
91. Nail clippers
92. Sandwich cookie (I tried it and it does work)
93. Interlocking plastic toy block
94. Carabiner
95. Compass
96. Pocket watch
97. Ratchet socket
98. Wine bottle cork
99. Nuts and bolts

ANATOMY OF A PENDULUM

* A weighted item that can be affixed to a line. May be pointed at the end, but this is optional.
* A line, such as a string or chain, from which the weight is suspended and can swing. The line should be flexible enough to allow for the motion of swinging.
* Enough space to hold the pendulum, while still facilitating the movement of the line and weight. A length of six to eight inches is sufficient. You can also add a bead or something decorative to hold onto.

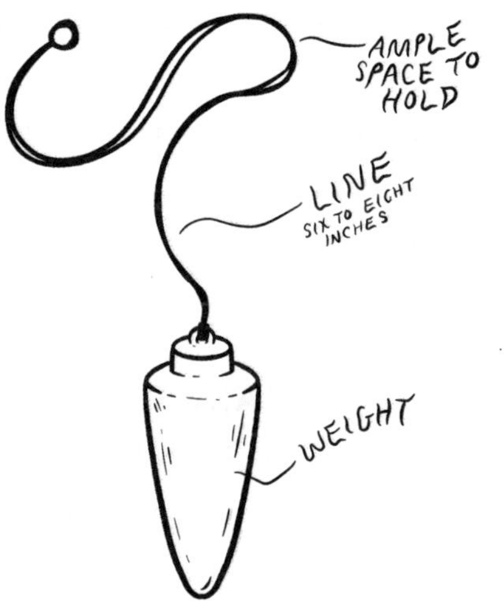

Other than these three basic points, the design and style of the pendulum is ultimately up to you! You can be as creative as you want, or you can keep it simple. The potential for what you can do is only limited by your own creativity.

Chapter 8

MAKING A PENDULUM

What if you don't want to just go and buy a pre-made pendulum? Making one's own tools is not only incredibly personal, but it can also be gratifying. There is often a big energetic difference in something that has been handmade by an individual, as opposed to something made by committee or in a factory. Making a pendulum may not be possible for everyone depending on access or ability, but if you want to try, here are some options!

POLYMER CLAY/OVEN-BAKE CLAY/AIR-DRY CLAY (OR CERAMIC, IF YOU HAVE A KILN)

Craft-store clay, be it oven-bake, air-dry, or another option, is usually a relatively easy and inexpensive option for making anything, including your own pendulum. Polymer oven-bake clay in particular is easy to work with, inexpensive, and doesn't really require more than an oven. You can get fancy with tools for shaping and carving if you choose, or you can just use your bare hands and kitchen utensils. These clays are available in a huge variety of colors and can be decorated with paints. You can make a hole near the top as part of your design, so that once it is cooled and ready to decorate (if you choose) you can thread a string through or attach a chain.

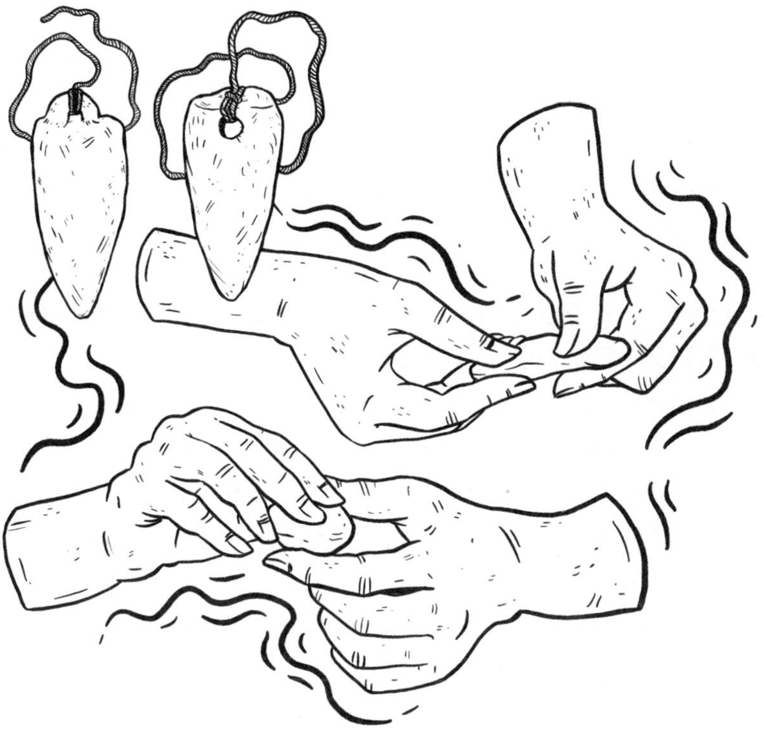

If you are or know a ceramics artist, you could make a pendulum out of clay and fire it. There are even metal clays that can be molded and worked with like clay, but when fired with a torch or a kiln, the binding material burns away, leaving only the metal. Working with materials that require firing in these kinds of ways can be limiting, but I hope this section may inspire a ceramics artist or a jeweler to try making something different and get a little witchy (and I'd love to see your creations if you do make your own).

To make a pendulum out of any kind of clay, shape the clay into your desired pendulum shape. This can be as simple or as complex as you choose.

Just make sure that you include a space to pass a string or chain through when you're done (such as a small loop or a hole punched through the clay). Finish the clay of your choice by following the instructions for that material, whether that means baking, drying, or firing.

ALUMINUM FOIL (OR "ALUMINIUM" FOR THOSE OUTSIDE OF NORTH AMERICA)

In Chapter 6 I mentioned that I made a pendulum out of aluminum foil to test the actual efficacy of aluminum as a material. I think that, in a pinch, an aluminum foil pendulum would serve a lot of people quite well. I don't think that it's ideal for healing, but I'd recommend it for divination. A bonus to using aluminum foil is that you can place other items inside of the foil, allowing you to build a pendulum around a small item, such as a crystal or a piece of wood. Aluminum foil is literally and figuratively a very flexible material to craft with.

You can experiment with different amounts of aluminum foil, depending on how big you would like the finished pendulum to be. I cut a piece about six inches long from a standard roll of foil. From there, you crumple the aluminum foil, shaping it into a pendulum shape. You can use pliers to compress the metal (be careful about compressing it too much, as the metal might start to rip). I shaped mine into a kind of elongated tear, with a sizeable "handle" at the top for the string. I chose a lighter string for this purpose, so that the pendulum would be heavier than the thread. Aluminum foil doesn't weigh very much, so you can get away with using sewing thread, or even a piece of hair (if your hair is long enough).

BEADS AND CHARMS

A good way to make a very intentional pendulum, and one that is personal to you and your needs, is to use beads and charms. You can choose any kind of beads or charms for this, even going so far as to mix and match different materials and styles to achieve different energetic traits. Using beads allows you to combine a few different crystals into one pendulum, or spell words of intention, or use color magic to channel a specific energy.

You can go about this in a couple of different ways:

* Thread the beads onto a string or wire. If you use a string, it can extend through the rest of your pendulum. If you use wire, shape a loop for the beads and then add a separate chain or string.

* Glue the beads together in a line, stacking them together, and then thread onto the chain or string.
* Thread beads onto a safety pin and affix a chain or string to the safety pin. I did this and I was happy with the result. I used letter beads to spell the word "heal," and added an iridescent star bead and a heart charm. It has some good 1990s DIY vibes, and it has a beautifully gentle energy.

CARVING/WHITTLING

If you find a piece of wood, or even stone, you like, you can carve your own pendulum. You'll need some specialized tools like a good knife, a small saw, and sandpaper, but you'll be able to get intimately involved with the item you're creating.

Some stone, such as soapstone, can be easily carved, and you can buy a kit to make this even easier. Carving stone generally takes a little bit more time and patience than carving wood, but the commitment and time you'll spend crafting will add intention to what you are creating. Just be careful with those carving tools.

SEWING

A textile pendulum is not something I've seen to date, but I think there could be potential for such a thing. If you have cats, they may be more interested in stealing it, but let's be real—with cats, pendulums are kind of a tempting item in the best of times. If your feline friends and familiars are anything like mine, you'll probably find your pendulums on the floor from time to time, regardless of the material from which they're made. If your pendulum is made from fabric, you can at least rest assured that it's not going to break if it falls on the floor.

Textiles hold a lot of space for magical potential. You can experiment with the magical correspondences of different textiles by looking into the plants or animals from which they come. You could dye the fabric you plan to use with intentionally selected plant dyes, or use color magic when selecting the fabric color. You can stuff that fabric with salt, or sand, or herbs. You can sew things into the form, such as crystals, or a piece of paper with something written or drawn on it. There are many options and opportunities for using textiles.

3-D PRINTING

The things I would do if I had a 3-D printer! Although I don't personally have experience creating magical tools with this technology, it would be a lot of fun, and there are models available on which to experiment.

OTHER MEDIUMS

I love a good trip to the hardware store, craft store, or thrift shop. You never know what's going to inspire you, and you can sometimes find inexpensive options that speak to you. Sometimes it's just what you need to get the creative juices flowing. Look at small objects both familiar and unfamiliar. Observe what connects with you. The materials you may find could surprise you.

At a hardware store you might be amazed to see the kinds of woods and metals that are available to you, and in forms that can be shaped into something new. Everything has potential to be magical, to become something intentional and personal.

Cast a pendulum out of resin. Forge one from metal. Use the skills you already have to make something special. Learn a new skill to make something different. You don't even have to source something new or do anything overly involved or complex. Wire-wrap that beloved crystal you already use every day. Repurpose an item from your altar. Use the necklace you wear every day. Get curious! Get playful. You might be surprised by what you end up conjuring into reality.

Storing Your Pendulum (or Pendulums)

The amount of decorum you put into storing your pendulums (or any magical tool, for that matter) is entirely up to you. In my own home, there is no rhyme or reason to how I store my pendulums. Some are hung up on the bulletin board above my desk. Others are placed with care on altar spaces. I believe that one is in a black velvet bag with a tarot deck. The way I store pendulums depends on how often I use them, or what I use them for. For example, the pendulum that I use for deciding on what essences to put in my coffee can usually be found in my kitchen area.

SOME THINGS TO CONSIDER:

* How often do you use the pendulum?
* Do you use the pendulum for one purpose? Is that purpose location sensitive?
* Is the pendulum made of something that might be affected by light?
* Is the pendulum fragile?
* How organized are you? Does organization matter to you?

If you have a lot of pendulums that you use for different purposes, you might be inclined to find a box with dividers in which you can store all your pendulums and keep them organized. This would also prevent the chains or strings from getting tangled. If you have one dedicated pendulum, you might keep it in a place of honor that keeps it safe until you need it. Perhaps you want to carry your pendulum with you every day. You might choose to have a small dish in which you can place the pendulum at night, ready to be put in your pocket or bag the next day. If you always use your pendulum in conjunction with pendulum boards, you might store your pendulum in a binder with all the pendulum boards you've copied or made. How you store your pendulum depends on your individual needs and wants. Don't make it any more difficult or complicated than it needs to be in order for you to access your pendulum for your purposes. Keep it as simple and/or magical as you want!

Part 3

PENDULUM MAGIC

Chapter 9

GETTING STARTED: AN INTRODUCTION TO PENDULUM BOARDS

When the pendulum is the right one for you, getting into the swing of things (pun intended) will be easier than you might expect. Don't overthink any of it. A pendulum is a tool that relies on you trusting yourself and the pendulum. You don't need to worry about doing anything "wrong" or making mistakes. Feeling uncertain? This section will help you get to know your pendulum, and help you become confident in developing a relationship with your magical tool.

CALIBRATING YOUR PENDULUM

Radiesthesist literature is full of information about "sensitivity tests," a way to determine the strength and reliability of results you'll get from using a pendulum. The "scoring" of these tests is based on how much a pendulum will gyrate while being held in a specific way. While I don't think this test has any level of reliable or helpful metrics, it is one way to determine if you're prone to autosuggestion; in other words, whether you are actively causing the pendulum to move. The same thing can be achieved by shifting your gaze away from the pendulum or closing your eyes while holding the pendulum. If the pendulum continues to swing in spite of the fact that you are no longer looking at it, then you know that its movement is coming more from something else, such as the true subconscious.

When you're getting started with a pendulum, you can calibrate it by sitting with it in a neutral space. Ask the pendulum to show you its movements for "yes," "no," and "maybe." You can also instruct the pendulum to swing a certain way to indicate certain answers, such as going east to west for "yes," north to south for "no," and swinging in a circle for "maybe." You may want to calibrate regularly for the first few readings to ensure that you're understanding the pendulum. If you notice that a certain pendulum's movements are always consistent, you can make note of them and remember them for future use.

Depending on what you're using a pendulum for, calibration might not be necessary. For example, if you're using it for healing or clearing, it might just swing in one way to accomplish its task. I find that I mostly use pendulums in a way in which they only need to gyrate in a circle, so I don't really need to calibrate them or interact with them to receive "yes" or "no" answers.

GETTING TO KNOW YOUR PENDULUM

Like tarot cards or other magical tools, you can spend as much or as little time as you want familiarizing yourself with your pendulum. Some people will perform introductory readings with their divination tools, by using a spread or series of questions that asks the tool about itself. This is a very animist approach, allowing the practitioner to get to know the item on its terms. It's entirely personal preference. I find that the best way to get to know a tool is simply by using it, but there is merit to communicating with it first. After calibrating and asking for its "yes," "no," and "maybe" movements, ask it simple yes and no questions. Trust your intuition here. Think of it like playing a game of Twenty Questions; you're just asking questions to get to know the pendulum and its energy. You can even ask the questions below, and then proceed based on the positive or negative responses the pendulum offers. From there, you can use a pendulum board to get more details.

When you break out a board to get more specific, you could ask it questions like:

* Do you have a name I can call you?
* Is there an ideal time to work with you?
* Is there a spirit connected to this pendulum?
* How can I best work with you?

PENDULUM BOARDS

When working with pendulums, you can receive more precise answers and information by using a pendulum board. There are a few types, depending on what you're trying to access, and there are a lot of fancy ones made of velvet, wood, or metal. These can be nice to have, but they're certainly not necessary. A piece of paper with the pendulum board drawn on it is effective, efficient, and accessible, and this is my go-to if I opt to use a pendulum board. At the end of this book, you'll find several pendulum boards for your use, including a blank one that you can fill in as you need. Convenient, *n'est-ce pas*?

Using a pendulum board is straightforward, but there is a bit more to interpret than "yes" and "no." Discerning what the pendulum is pointing to on a board can require a few more steps, and that can take some practice. With some time and effort, you'll be interpreting clear messages and answers in no time.

Circular Board

When people talk about pendulum boards, this is usually what they're referring to. A circular board has possible answers arranged in a circle, sometimes with arrows drawn across the center. The words are often repeated, with "yes" being across from "yes," so that it is very clear as to what the pendulum is trying to communicate. These boards say "yes," "no," and "maybe," and some include other words like "wait" or "rephrase."

Some of these boards also have the alphabet and some numbers written or printed around the outer edge, so that the pendulum can also communicate words, not unlike a spirit board. The pendulum may communicate a specific letter by swinging in its direction (in which case you can ask "Did you mean this letter?" and have the pendulum indicate "yes" or "no"). You could also hold the pendulum over each letter so that it can vibrate or gyrate over its selection. Communicating with a pendulum this way can take a lot of patience.

Half-Circle Board

This is a very helpful and efficient way of getting information from a pendulum. The half-circle boards are exactly what they sound like: a half-circle divided into a number of slices, each with a word, number, or letter on it. The pendulum is held at the center of the straight edge, and when the question is asked, the pendulum will swing to one of the slices. These types of boards allow you to get an answer based on several choices, rather than having to narrow things down by asking "yes" or "no" questions, or having

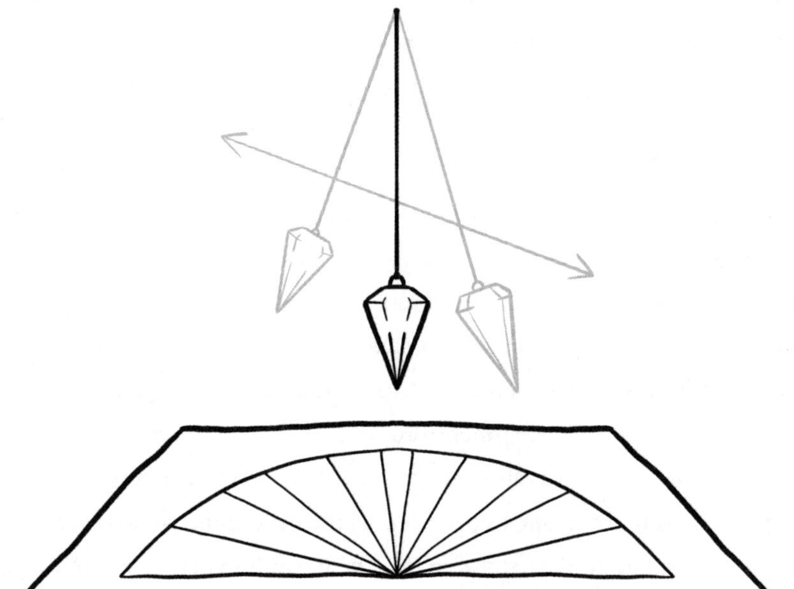

the pendulum spell out words, one letter at a time. This can be a helpful tool if you're trying to make a decision or organize your life. You can draw a half-circle and fill out the spaces with the possible options, from which the pendulum can indicate the best choice. I used this type of board during a past-life reading I was doing for myself. Using the half-circle board, I was able to write out options for information about my past life, like number of years and decades, places, and so on. I was able to discern a lot of information more quickly than I would have otherwise. The half-circle is certainly my favorite type of pendulum board, and if I'm going to use a board, I'm most likely to use or make one of these.

Spirit Board

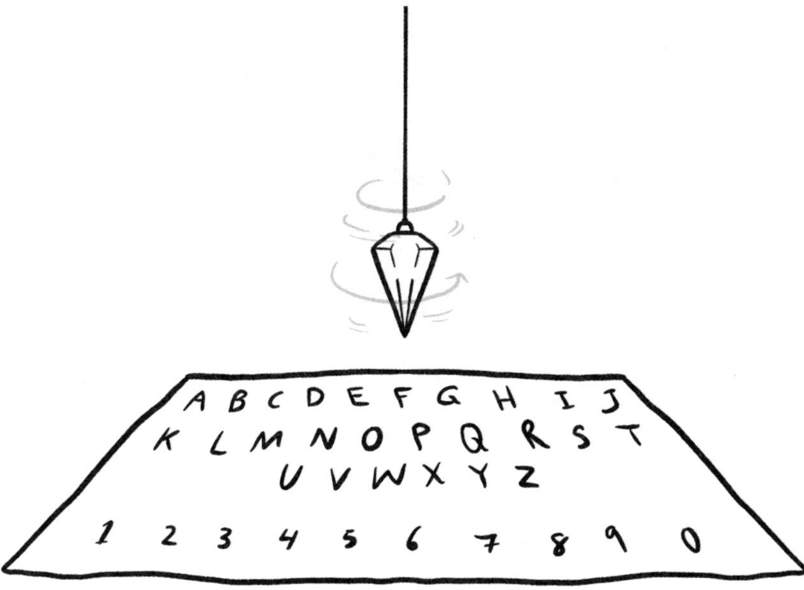

You can use an actual spirit board (like a Ouija board) as a pendulum board. Spirit boards are usually a very readable size, so you can more easily determine which letter the pendulum is vibrating or gyrating over. It's not necessarily ideal, because the process is still slow, but it can be helpful if you're getting the impression that the pendulum wishes to communicate something beyond "yes" or "no."

You might find that a pendulum board of any kind is ideal for you, and that it makes your readings easier and more concise. Pendulums are so personal and individualized, and that goes for the reading process, too. Some (like me) might find that pendulum boards don't remotely serve them or benefit them. Others might find that the pendulum board is the perfect tool, and that using it is a snap. It's entirely up to you to determine what works for you.

Chapter 10

EXPERIMENT AND PLAY/ PLAY AND EXPERIMENT

There is enough in this world that is serious. There is enough in this world that is rigid. There is enough in life that is going to tell you what to do and how to do it. Your magical practice should be an opportunity to escape, to reconnect with yourself, with nature, with the ethereal and unknown. Never be afraid to experiment—give yourself the grace and room to play. Welcome in spontaneity and silliness and curiosity. You are allowed to smile, to laugh at yourself, to ask questions of yourself and the world you live in. Give yourself space to be something other than what society asks (or tells) you to be.

I'm not a fan of any organized religion, and that applies to paths of witchcraft. On paper, there's nothing wrong with following a written text, or following the advice of a teacher or leader. However, it can quickly degrade into hierarchy, unnecessary rules, and reinforcement of structures and ideas that witchcraft should be critical of and resistant to. I can't stress enough how dangerous it is to fall into someone else's dogma and take their every word as gospel. At the end of the day, any form of spirituality is based on the thoughts, ideas, and agendas of fallible humans. We as humans are divine in our own ways, but we are not divine beings. We are mortal entities;

complicated souls living in animal bodies. We are incredibly complex. The only path that is right for any of us is our own path. We need to make our own decisions and be free to exist in the way that is best for us.

The practice of witchcraft is a choose your own adventure. It's fairly open to picking and choosing, becoming tailor-made to each individual practitioner. You can do whatever you want. That doesn't mean that you should do whatever you want, or that there won't be consequences. Indeed, there is a possibility that the choices you make may affect others, and vice versa. This shouldn't be a limitation.

Consider an art practice. The formation of an art practice—be it painting, writing, acting, dancing, whatever medium—is a natural process. It is fed by conscious and unconscious influences and inspirations. One will seek out inspirations, instruction, and motivation, but they will also be forever influenced by subconscious forces, societal forces, individual politics, and morality, among other things. The formation of a magical practice is the same, and like the creation of art, it is necessary to include an aspect of experimentation and play alongside research and hard work.

There was a time when I felt pressured to practice my witchcraft in a particular way. I experienced the same thing in my creative art practices. I found myself growing stagnant in my practices because I was concerned that I wasn't doing it "the right way." As I've grown and gotten older, I've learned the fallacy that is the notion of a "right way." There is no universal right way. There is no one-size-fits-all solution that works for every individual. There is no one answer for all humans. Again: we are very complex. The human species is a mosaic of differences and variations. It's part of what makes us so interesting. It's also what makes people turn on each other so easily. We get too hung up on the right way, the wrong way, my way, your way. Humans are really good at judging each other, in spite of the fact that we are communal animals who rely on each other for survival. We find flaws in each other, and let other people's influence cause us to find flaws in ourselves. The influence of other humans is inescapable, but efforts can be made in small ways to allow ourselves to find who we are as individuals. It's difficult, but it's worth trying to untangle our perception of ourselves from others' perceptions of us. If we can't try to untangle those perceptions within the safe space of our own thoughts, within the space of our spirituality or magic, where can we find space to do so? The practice of magic can be a safe space; something to escape to when things are difficult. As such, it makes sense to try to make it a space that is personal, free of judgment, and free of structure.

Let yourself play. Let yourself experiment. Give yourself space to ask "What if I do this?" or "What will happen if . . . ?" Let yourself be curious, inquisitive, and free from judgment. Quiet the voice in your head that criticizes you for trying to do something different. Ignore the voice in your mind that tries to tell you that you are making a mistake, that you will be judged, that something bad will happen. Give yourself the chance to explore, to try something different.

People talk a lot about healing the inner child, but sometimes I think that we just need to *listen* to our inner child. What would the young you do? What would you have done as a kid? For a child, would the answer be so obvious and set in stone? Would you stop a child from playing? Would you criticize a child for asking questions, or getting muddy, or playing make-believe? Hopefully the answer is no. If you were prevented from such things as a child, I am sorry. But this is an opportunity to heal that part of you, to access the curiosity you were deprived of.

You are meant to play.

You are meant to experiment.

Start now.

High Vibrations and High Frequencies

Throughout communities of people who talk about the metaphysical, there are often conversations around having a "high vibration" or a "high frequency." I encountered some of this while researching this book, and I think that it's important to address. First of all, what does this really mean? Unfortunately, it's not easily defined. The concept of "high vibrations" feels like one of those things within the metaphysical world that is intentionally cryptic in order to keep people questioning themselves, which in turn takes away their power.

Technically, everything has a vibration, just as everything emits small amounts of radiation or energy. The physical world breaks down to the tiniest structures, with atoms moving and vibrating. All matter is made up of atoms, with different numbers of electrons and neutrons forming different elements. The structure of the atoms indicates whether the substance is a liquid, solid, or gas—they move and shift, functioning on a whole other spectrum than we ourselves can possibly imagine. I do believe in vibrations, and that every individual person has a specific energy and vibration. I'm just a bit weary of how people talk about it, and how ideas of vibrational energy can be (and are) weaponized to make people feel small or incapable. This is especially worrisome, because the reality is, the only things that absolutely lower one's vibration are hatred and cruelty. The rest is . . . relative.

When people discuss vibrations, they talk more about how one feels, and how to raise one's vibration. If you go to an internet search engine and type in "high vibration," you'll find thousands of blogs, videos, and articles about how to raise your vibration. Very few include information on why this matters, or what the end goal should be. After all, how can you truly raise your vibration? The result cannot be guaranteed. An individual's vibration can't be measured or tested, and if anyone tells you otherwise, I feel like you should steer clear. Rhetoric around high vibrations quickly disintegrates under scrutiny, revealing that it is a system built on privilege and victim blaming.

I am not here to cut anyone down for practicing a certain way, but one of my mottos in life is "question everything." It was only when I claimed my own power that I really started to uncover the truths I needed to know. There are no real teachers in magic. You can only take what you need from someone and leave the rest. You can't let yourself get tangled up in anyone's dogma.

I largely reject the idea of high vibrations and high frequencies, because it is too easy to pull the thread and unravel the problems. I'm more interested in fostering auras in which others can feel safe and secure; to make your energetic space one that others (physical or spiritual) would like to spend some time in. Think of your energy, your vibration, your frequency, as your home. It doesn't matter what your home is. It could be a shoebox of memories that you take solace in, or a big house with everything you've ever dreamed of. But if the space isn't inviting, you won't be able to convince anyone to enter that space. Sometimes that space will be inviting to like-minded people, but others who don't share your worldview may think it's dirty and disgusting. You can't please anyone, but you can do your best to make your energetic space a home. If it's home to you, it will be home to the people you are meant to connect with.

In discussions about pendulums, people may talk about having a high vibration because it welcomes in spirits and energies that are like them. The "law of attraction" becomes a buzz phrase. Like attracts like, so if you put out the energy you want, it will come back to you. It's all really just a sympathetic magic. If the goal in divination is to invite in spirits and energies, I believe it's a better avenue to be authentic, and to open up your heart and space to whoever has messages. It's not always up to us who or what will come through when divining. We don't get to choose who needs us. Why run the risk of making some spirits feel unwelcome? Why try to make yourself into something you're not? The goal should be authenticity and honesty.

Chapter 11

GETTING THE RIGHT ANSWERS

In *A Witches' Bible: The Complete Witches' Handbook*, Janet and Stewart Farrar describe divination as "clairvoyance using tools," and discuss how these tools, like tarot cards, I Ching, tea leaves, or any other "prop," act as a trigger to the intuition. What this means is that our intuition, our psychic-ness, is always present and ready to go, but sometimes we need tools or aids to help us tap into, and activate, our intuition.

"Trigger" is kind of a loaded word these days, especially in psychological terms, referring to a stimuli that causes painful memories to surface. Because of this, it may be difficult for some to look at the concept of an intuition trigger and feel totally comfortable with that terminology. "Trigger" can feel like it's inherently negative. Instead, we can choose to use words like "spark" or "activator." It's really up to the individual and what feels comfortable.

I like the term "spark" because it brings to mind a sensation of curiosity and excitement. A spark feels joyful and driven, with a tiny note of danger. In terms of intuition, it doesn't mean that the downloads or messages received from that spark won't be negative or difficult. After all, a single spark can burn down an entire forest.

An intuition trigger or spark can be anything. It can be a tool, but it can also be a specific scent, place, or another person's energy. I find that being outdoors communing with plants is a huge intuitive spark for me. There's something about talking to and spending time with plants that unlocks a lot of knowing and messages.

This book is about pendulums and other things that exist in the peripherals of that central focus. Yes, pendulums can be intuition triggers, allowing diviners to tap into or unlock those inner workings that allow us to receive messages and information from the aether. Pendulums can be useful for this because of how simple and straightforward they are (or, at least, they seem to be). Simple tools like pendulums can be enough to spark the intuition, allowing you to tap into what questions need to be asked (and asking them in the right way), whether a board should be brought into the mix, or what further work needs to be done to get the best reading. Often with intuition, once the floodgates open, a lot of incredible stuff will come through.

What is the best way to spark your intuition? It's really up to you to explore, experiment, and play, in order to see what will work the best for you. It might not be a pendulum, but you might find that using a pendulum in conjunction with other tools is helpful. You might find that a tarot deck works the best for you. Perhaps a crystal ball or scrying mirror gets the job done. It's entirely your preference, and what feels most comfortable. And, of course, lean into whatever seems to yield the best results. Ironically, it's essential that you just trust your intuition with these things. No one can tell you what's going to be best for you in terms of creating comfortable situations that allow you to spark your intuition. It is ultimately personal. I often reflect on the concept of divination, and of looking for signs and symbols in the world. I'm not of the belief that everything is a divine intervention, and I'm not of the belief that everything is a random sign. I choose to actively observe the world around me, and that results in seeing patterns or recognizing synchronicities (meaningful coincidences). There is always information around us that we can internalize or interpret, and while I believe in divine timing, I don't believe that everything needs to be meaningful.

ANSWERS VS. GUIDANCE

There is a difference between divining for answers and divining for guidance. The two are not entirely exclusive, but there is an important distinction. Constantly looking for answers outside of oneself, especially in terms of divination, can be a way of removing responsibility. When we look for answers, we are often seeking explanation, justification, or even a heads-up of what's to come (if one is using divination to try to look toward the future). Demanding answers is borne from a sense of entitlement, coming from a place that the spirits, deities, ancestors, or the universe somehow owe you information. When talking about looking for answers, I'm not talking about day-to-day answers for real-life questions. I'm talking about constantly looking for explanation as to why you are where you are in this present moment. I'm talking about the "why, god???" moments, when there's nothing exactly unmanageable or impossible, but there's a sense that things "should" be easier or more manageable, all the while refusing help, not doing the work, and not listening to the answers and information that are already being presented to you.

There's nothing wrong with looking for, or asking for, answers. We all feel lost sometimes. But when we ask for answers as a means of removing responsibility from ourselves, it's not productive, and it's a misuse of the craft of divination.

When we use divination as a way to ask for guidance, we can accept responsibility for where we are and what's going on in our lives, but we are acknowledging that we can't do it alone. We are asking for help, for direction, for clues on how to proceed. The reality is, we usually have the answers we need, just by existing and living our lives. If you hold an awareness of yourself, others, and your world, you can access any information you would actually need to improve or make changes, or whatever one does with guidance.

We are not meant to have all of the answers, but we are also not meant to go it alone, without support. Divination is best when it's used as a support system.

I use divination predominantly to ask for guidance, to open up my intuition and myself to certain opportunities within a day, or to avoid others. I use it as a gentle compass, where, at the end of the day, I take full responsibility for myself and my choices. After all, why would anyone not want to feel in control of their lives? It's the goal for most of us. Most of us want nothing more than to be able to make choices, exercise our free will, and do whatever we want for our best highest good (within the confines of generally accepted morality and the laws of physics).

ASKING QUESTIONS THE RIGHT WAY

There is the notion of asking questions the "right way." Divination is not a precise science, but it is a situation where precision must be exercised when asking questions. The Spirits (or whoever/whatever you contact when divining) are incredibly flexible with a lot of things, but they tend to be very literal when it comes to wording. The clearer and more specific the question, the better. A twist! This isn't really my opinion. It's based on the ideas of others who have written about divination, especially in relation to pendulums. Do you actually need to be that specific? Will the Spirits give you weird or inaccurate answers based on wording? How do they feel about Oxford commas?

Precision has its place, but I'm not convinced that divination, or magic as a whole, is it. Divination is spiritual. It is an emotional practice. It is not scientific. Its function is entirely theoretical, and how we interpret any of it is based on our own individual experience. If you ask three different tarot readers the same question, you will get three different readings. Every time you ask the same question, you have already changed in some way. You're already thinking about the first time you asked that question and the answer you received. That influences the next reading, and the next. Divination is deeply personal, and even when someone else is reading for us, our own interpretation of their reading shapes that very reading. In fact, the experience of the reader and the receiver will be completely different, even though they're sharing something. No two people on the planet have the same experience, no matter how closely shared it is. The way we experience anything is influenced by a whole mosaic of different factors, and that's why art, music, and divination can be interpreted in so many different ways.

Of course, if you're asking vague questions, you'll get vague answers. When you go into a reading, whether it's on your own or given by someone else, the experience will meet you where you are. You will get out of it what you put into it. If you go into it feeling skeptical and uncertain, or you're just not feeling it that day, your reading will match that. So, it's really not about the questions you're asking, but more about the energy you're bringing, and the confidence you have when you're beginning the reading. Spirits will meet you where you're at, and that includes making space and accommodations for you as a person. As long as you trust that you're going to receive good information, you typically will. The entities you connect with through your readings (even if it's simply your subconscious) aren't here to mess with you or complicate your life. Humans do stuff like that. Ethereal and non-corporeal beings, your subconscious, god, whoever, whatever, are not interested in misleading you. That's what makes divination so wonderful. It's never going to readily be dishonest, because divination doesn't have an agenda.

You don't have to be crystal clear. You don't have to plan your questions ahead of time. You don't have to be afraid that the messages you receive are going to be needlessly misleading or dishonest. Whoever/whatever is on the other end of the pendulum, or the cards, or the crystal ball, is not interested in any of that, and it will always understand your intention and what you really mean. Divinatory tools are there to help you connect to your true self, so of course they're going to understand what you mean, even when you can't properly bring to words what your question is. Not all of us are good at putting questions or feelings into words. Not all of us are verbal. Divination is divine. Divine things don't put limitations on us based on our ability, or who we are. Divine things meet us where we are, and make room for us on our terms, and based on our needs.

When asking any questions of any divinatory tools, all that matters is that you feel good. "Good" is really subjective here. Good can mean calm, collected, neutral, having enough spoons, rested, energetic . . . anything that is neutral, or more on the side of positive than not.

TIMING

There are some notions that the timing must be correct to use a pendulum. One radiesthesist suggests that the best times to use a pendulum are seven to eleven in the morning, three to five in the evening, eight to eleven at night, immediately after a rain shower, or on a cloudy day. In *Solitary Witch,* Silver RavenWolf suggests that a good time to practice dowsing or pendulum magic is when Mars conjuncts the Moon.

There might be some validity to holding to these times, but I'm a big "do the thing when you need to" person. I don't always follow my own advice, but sometimes you just need to do the divination or do the spell, even if the timing isn't exactly optimal. Sometimes it's best to go with the feeling that is telling you that the timing is right. I have found great success in utilizing lunar or solar timing to do particular magic, but there's nothing quite like striking while the iron is hot.

Doubt is the enemy of divination. It really doesn't matter where you are (short of maybe standing next to an electromagnet, or a full-on transmitter, or something else you might not have much business standing next to). The pendulum will serve its purpose. However, if you're feeling unsure, or uncomfortable, or weary, you will find that your reading experience is less than favorable, or simply unhelpful. The only "bad" time to divine is when you aren't clearheaded. Divination or spellwork is a very dodgy thing to do if you're not feeling focused or grounded. It is never exactly wise to do anything, magical or mundane, when you're feeling especially riled up, anxious, upset, angry, or unwell. Consider this: if you wouldn't operate heavy machinery in your current state, opt out of doing anything magical. Do not engage with the cards. Do not pick up the pendulum. Do not send that text message. Take hold of a crystal, pet a cat, drink some water, go for a walk.

A time when you're feeling upset in any way is not the time to engage with magical tools. You will not get the answers you seek. Even if you are not the one doing the reading, your energy will come through, and the information, the messages, will become muddy and unclear. Consider any time you've been especially distraught. Maybe you couldn't form the right words to express your feelings. Maybe you were triggered, managing shock, or trauma, and you really just needed to re-ground and re-center yourself.

There is no rush. You shouldn't feel pressured to override your primary feelings to try to get information that you might not even want to hear. Stress and the magical do not mix. It gets messy. Yes, use magical tools to help ground yourself. Lean into the care and compassion of animal familiars (or just the animals you live around), plant and herbal allies, and crystals. Make tea, use gem essences, craft with tinctures and essences, read a healing book. Times of difficulty don't always need explanation right away. In fact, they rarely do. It can be tempting to lean into divination, in hopes of making sense of something, whether it is annoying or traumatic. But even if the divination provides the right information, you may not be able to process it. You may not even want to hear it. My spouse and I have started asking, "Do you need answers, or do you just need to vent?" when one of us, or a friend, is upset. Sometimes we just need to be heard, and we just need to feel held. Sometimes we don't need solutions or more ideas or answers of any kind. We just need to be.

Electrical Interference

As I write this, the power is out on my street. I write my first drafts with a typewriter, so a power outage doesn't provide much excuse to not work. I sit at my desk, the hum of vehicles from the outside invading my room, as a team of electricians works to repair a power pole on my street. I think about how pendulums are said to work better (or at least, it's heavily implied) when there is little to no electrical influence. The less electricity, the better. Most of the books that say this were not written in the twenty-first century. A lot of the theory around dowsing, radiesthesia, and divination were written when electricity was still limited, at least in relation to our world now. When these books were being written, lights and appliances were pretty much the only things in the home that used electricity, and they were easily turned off. Even telephones of the past were not reliant on electricity. Electricity is all but woven into the fabric of our everyday lives. Electricity and technology constantly demand our attention. No wonder our reliance on these things and their constant presence in our lives makes some people feel physically sick. No wonder we feel better when we escape all of it for a minute. I'm not saying that life is better without electricity or technology. Both are valuable tools, offering a lot to our lives, from how we learn to how we socialize . . . it's kind of fantastic. There are countless people I never would have met if it wasn't for technology. Electricity (as it all boils down to, really) is a priceless tool and asset that makes our lives easier. But, as with anything, there can be a limit to how good something is, or how often it should be in our lives. Take divination and witchcraft, for example. One could debate whether technology is a benefit or a detriment to our craft. It is all borne of magic conceived long ago (though some is more recent than you might think). Would magic and divination work better if we were not surrounded by electricity? Or have we simply learned to adapt, the way we adapt to everything? Adaptability is a key component in magical history and magical theory. It's that idea of figuring out what works and what doesn't. Simplifying. Restructuring. Reconsidering. Acknowledging that what does work for one person may not work for another, and may not work for you. Magic and divination are not one-size-fits-all. Few things are. In fact, maybe nothing is.

Chapter 12

CLEARING AND HEALING WITH PENDULUMS

The use of pendulums to clear and heal has its roots in radiesthesia, but the concept is quite sound beyond the practice. The object of energetic clearing and/or healing is to neutralize or remove unwanted energies, and allow space for new, welcome energies to enter. It can help elevate the feeling of a room, lifting up spirits of those in the space (or within the body). Practices like Reiki, acupuncture, EFT (emotion freedom technique) tapping, crystal healing, sound baths, and others are examples of energetic healing; all work with different vibrations and energies in order to let energy flow. These techniques are all very different, but at their core the goal is similar: get the "bad" stuff out, so you can invite the good in. Whether you are healing a body or a space, the principles are the same.

CLEARING VERSUS CLEANSING

In this section, I talk mostly about clearing, because clearing isn't quite as intense as cleansing. Pendulums are less suited to fully cleansing a space, because they're not quite powerful enough. However, they can clear a space or a body quite well.

Clearing is energetic tidying. Picture your psyche as a messy desk. It doesn't take a lot to organize everything and create a free surface on which you can do your work. When you place your pencils in a jar and file away your papers, you're not completely rolling up your sleeves to do a deep spring clean, but maybe you're eliminating some of the clutter and doing a little dusting. Think of the term "clear your mind." You're just moving away from what isn't serving you right now, so that you can better focus on the task at hand. It can be a mental or emotional break. Activities like meditation or forest baths can help you clear your mind and your energetic self, providing a sense of relief in an otherwise hectic and chaotic world.

Cleansing is an energetic deep clean. You're wiping the baseboards and washing the curtains. You're completely neutralizing a space so that you can start from scratch and invite in more suitable energies. It's a more intense experience, and to do a really deep energetic cleanse, you'll need to put in a lot of work.

Clearing can be done to a space or a person, but cleansing is only for spaces. Both can be achieved by physically and literally cleaning. A shower can help clear the day from your mind and energetic space. Washing the floors and organizing the cabinets will physically and energetically cleanse. The mundane can be magic!

PENDULUM CLEARING 101

Stand in the space and let yourself feel the room. Notice the vibes. How does the space feel? How do you feel? Are pets behaving differently in the space? Are you avoiding being in that certain space? You can use a pendulum at this point to interact with the space and assess what needs to be done.

In feng shui (the Chinese art of organizing a space to harmonize with the individuals in it), some practitioners use pendulums to diagnose the space, as well as use the pendulum to remove detrimental energy.

Once you've determined what room (or rooms) need to cleared, choose a pendulum that is well suited to absorbing and/or transforming energies. Good choices would include black tourmaline, amethyst, black kyanite (also very good for healing the energetic body), selenite, onyx, or crystal quartz. Let the pendulum swing in a circle, radiating the energy of the crystal outward. A crystal pendulum can act as kind of an energetic water filter. It can suck up the unwanted stuff, but it is also capable of radiating the energy of the stone into the space. Move about the space, letting the pendulum do its thing, until you feel like the work is done.

Witch Tip

When clearing or cleansing, have at least one window or door open. You'll want to let things out, and if the space is sealed, it's going to be more challenging. This is *essential* if you are also planning on warding (protecting) the space after you cleanse it. If you don't, you run the risk of sealing up the bad stuff inside, which is kind of a waste of all that energy you just put in!

When you're done, cleanse the pendulum and recharge it. You might also light some incense that invites in the kind of energy you'd like to cultivate in the space, and place helpful crystals with the same goal.

Using a Pendulum to Clear or Cleanse Crystals

This has become my favorite way to clear and cleanse crystals. Place the crystal in front of you and dangle your pendulum above it. The pendulum will start swinging in a circle. Different crystals will cause the pendulum to swing in larger or smaller circles, depending on the energy. Let the pendulum do its thing. After a few moments, the pendulum will wind down and cease swinging until it's hanging motionless above the crystal. Once it's still, the crystal is cleansed. It's that easy! Each crystal is different, so some will take longer to cleanse than others. I really like this technique because it uses your own energy, but it's also very visual, and removes a lot of guesswork from the process. It also helps form a sense of familiarity between you and the stone.

You can use any pendulum you wish for this process, but something that is already well suited to clearing and cleansing is a good choice. I've found that amethyst works really well for the stones I am cleansing.

Your understanding of your pendulum will indicate what the different size of circles mean. The speed of swings may also offer you information. My pendulum swings in big circles when something needs work or needs to be cleared. The smaller the circle, the less energy that is being held in the subject. When the pendulum is swinging in small, slow circles, it might still need to be cleared, but it's not as pressing as something that is causing the pendulum to swing in big, fast circles.

PENDULUM HEALING 101

Please note that this section is not intended to diagnose or offer replacements for medical treatment or advice.

Sometimes we experience things that are painful or difficult to manage, and there is only so much that can be done "practically." There are sensations that are difficult to diagnose. Sometimes the physical pain that we feel is emotional, and trauma does live in the body. For example, because of my special brand of neurodivergence, I get pain flare-ups whenever I'm stressed. There's no reason for it, beyond the fact that that my body is registering pain signals because of the stress and anxiety I'm feeling. When I give myself an opportunity to calm down, the pain subsides. Utilizing forms of energetic healing can help. Energetic healing is also helpful in terms of emotional or mental well-being, where other forms of therapy or counseling just aren't giving you what you need. I get as much benefit from metaphysical and energetic practices as I do traditional therapy (and I do both).

Using a pendulum to heal yourself can be difficult, but it is not impossible. Pendulum healing is done the same way as clearing, but instead of doing so in a room, you are doing so over parts of your body. The pendulum can also be used to help pinpoint where there may be blockages that are causing discomfort or difficulty. Pay attention to what the pendulum is doing when you hover it over different parts of your body. If it starts swinging, that is likely a spot that needs attention. The pendulum can be used over that spot to clear it, or other work can be done. This work can be crystal healing, or another form of energetic healing, but it can also be an opportunity to go to a massage therapist, do some yoga, or apply a compress. Physical healing can unblock energy as much as energetic healing, and sometimes it is the answer.

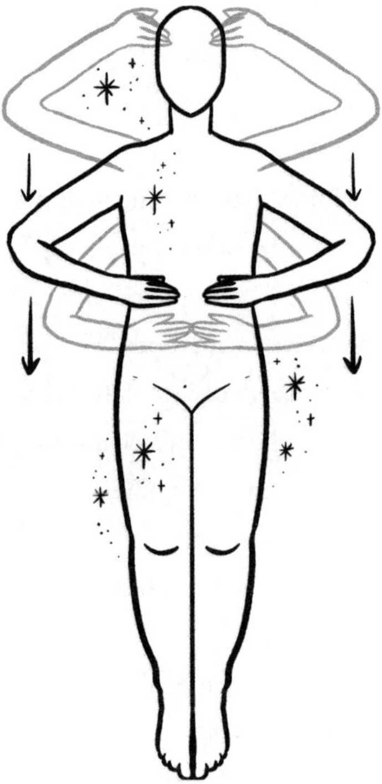

Remember to listen to your body. If you're experiencing physical pain or discomfort, take care of yourself, and consider seeing a professional. But if you're just kind of feeling mentally or emotionally rough, energetic healing can be a good place to start.

Body Scanning with a Pendulum

A body scan is essentially a way to connect with your body on an energetic level, and to become more aware of how your body is feeling. There are many guided meditations to help do this, but it's quite straightforward and you can do it on your own. Personally, I find meditation (or any kind of sitting still) to be difficult, so I put on binaural beats or trance-inducing music in the background. It provides just enough background noise to help me filter out the noises in my house, and in my head. The meditation timer on the app Insight Timer is very good for this.

There are many different ways to do body scans, but I'll share what works for me, and then how I take it to the next level by using a pendulum. I even did a body scan and pendulum scan on my cat (he seemed pretty happy about it, and he's a very salty old man).

Start by getting comfortable. Eliminate possible distractions (for example, putting your phone on silent or removing it from the space could be helpful). Maybe have a drink of water, put on comfy clothes, throw on your background noise (if you choose). I like to get comfy in a sitting position on my bed, but you can also lie down, sit up on a yoga mat, or stand in a quiet spot—whatever allows you to get comfortable, mindful, and have some quiet time. Once you're feeling relaxed and content, start by sitting with your body for a moment. Just breathe, and bring awareness to your body on a whole. Sit in your body for a moment, and clear your mind of distractions and concerns. Just be.

To begin, I recommend just using your hands. Cup your palms slightly, as if holding water. This will give you a chance to get familiar with your own body and its energies. When you're ready, hold your hands over your body. Start at the top of your head and scan downward. I find it helpful to use my hands to scan over my body, hovering my hands above each of my chakras for a short while, or moving my hands over parts of my body that have been giving me trouble. Body scans give us an opportunity to pay attention to parts of our bodies that we might not normally. I often find myself surprised at what I encounter when I take the time to do a body scan. During today's scan, for example, I found that I felt some "sticky" energy (for lack of a better term) around my Manipura, the solar plexus chakra. The solar plexus is the focal point for our will and personal power, so when it's weak or blocked, it can manifest as micromanaging, struggling with minute details, and an inability to bring things to fruition. This is exactly what I've been struggling with, but I didn't really take the time to acknowledge it otherwise.

Once you've completed the body scan, you can take steps to unblock or clear any chakras and do healing around those areas. There is also a distinct possibility that you won't feel anything, and that means that you're doing well, with no areas for concern or focus. Not a bad place to be! (Of course, if you think there's something really wrong, it never hurts to get a second opinion.)

Once you're familiar with your own energy, you can bring in a pendulum. For a full-body scan with a pendulum, you may find it more comfortable to lie down on your back, hovering the pendulum over your body. Pay attention to the pendulum's movements as you move it down your body, focusing on your chakra points. When I do these kinds of scans, I find that the pendulum will typically stay fairly still or swing weakly over points that don't need work, but will swing in big circles over the areas that need attention. I like to use a pendulum after a body scan with my hands, because it can confirm what I already know, but it also presents an opportunity to use the pendulum to help unravel the fussy areas a bit, opening them up as if working out a knot in a muscle. This helps clear the individual chakras and contributes to balancing out the chakra system as a whole.

The key to body scanning with or without a pendulum is to pay attention to your body, and to not be afraid to spend a lot of time listening and feeling. Take your time. A body scan is an opportunity to connect with yourself and become more aware of this body you inhabit.

Commonplace Books: An Argument in Favor of Journaling and Note-Taking

From the Renaissance up until about the nineteenth century, many individuals would keep something called a commonplace book. This was a place for everything, without being too much of a diary. Instead of keeping day-to-day thoughts and records, a commonplace book would hold everything else, from notes to formulas to recipes to letters to quotes. Think of a bullet journal, where everything is useful information, categorized to be easily found and utilized, but unspecific to one particular theme or part of life. Commonplace books have less to do with thoughts or maintaining chronology. Commonplace books are all of the ephemera and general information that one finds useful in day-to-day life.

On paper, a commonplace book is a lot like a grimoire or book of shadows, but one big difference is that a commonplace book might be more likely to have notes of failures, or something that didn't work. Many magical texts are started by an individual copying everything from another's book, word for word. There's an expected level of precision, reminiscent of medieval monks copying down texts into illuminated manuscripts. A commonplace book has the potential to be full of trials and errors, with notes about failures as well as successes. One can only expect to truly learn by having space to make mistakes and figure out what went wrong.

The concept of journaling comes up a lot in magical and occult spaces, so it can become a bit annoying and can start to feel redundant, but journaling is helpful. I can't count the number of times I've read contemporary magical texts that offer practices that boil down to "journal and meditate" as a alternative to spellwork and a form of self-care. Okay. Thanks. Do I believe that journaling fixes everything? Absolutely *not*! But I'll be the first to admit that journaling (and meditation) are helpful. I do get annoyed when it's one of the only points of discussion, because the addition of journaling can start to blur the lines between magical practice and self-help, which is justifiable, but not always helpful. I do feel better when I've started my day with a tarot card pull and a little bit of writing, and I do find a twenty-minute brain dump onto paper to be helpful. It's just a way for us to clear our minds and let things out, instead of rattling around in our brains.

I am not talking about journaling in the sense of brain dumping or airing grievances onto the page. I'm talking about it more in the sense of having a record of what one has done. While working with a pendulum or any type of magical tool or system, I recommend taking notes. Journal about your experience, make notes about what worked and what didn't. Make a record of your journey, and give yourself a reference to learn from. Every magical practice is deeply personal, so it makes sense to be aware of your own practice. The magical world does have space for the scientific method, and you might be amazed at what you learn and what works for you. In chaos magic (a very do-it-yourself approach to magic), practitioners pay close attention to what does and doesn't work, which makes for a results-based type of magic. The idea is that all magic is possible, but if it doesn't work, that could be because the approach or the method wasn't correct. In alchemical practices of old, the alchemists were scientists who recorded not only what happened, but how it made them feel. Keeping a record of everything you do in your magical practice can be a useful tool as you grow and evolve.

Chapter 13

THE CHAKRAS

The chakras are energy centers in your body that can become unbalanced or blocked, which can then cause physical or energetic upsets or difficulty. They can be rebalanced through different types of energetic healing, including Reiki and crystal healing. A pendulum can be used to determine any blockages or difficulties around the chakras and can also help unwind the energy a bit in order to allow flow. This chapter is meant to help you understand the seven major chakras, should you choose to use a pendulum to work with them.

The first known written mention of the chakras dates from roughly 700–500 BCE. The chakras are energy centers that affect our physical body, as well as our psychological, emotional, and spiritual selves. There are seven main chakras, with each one ruling over a different part of our body. Each chakra is a different color and elemental ruling, and can be worked with through the sympathetic magic of using like colors, crystals, or roots.

In my experience, utilizing the chakra system is the most effective way to access energetic healing, and using a pendulum in conjunction with the chakras is very potent and powerful.

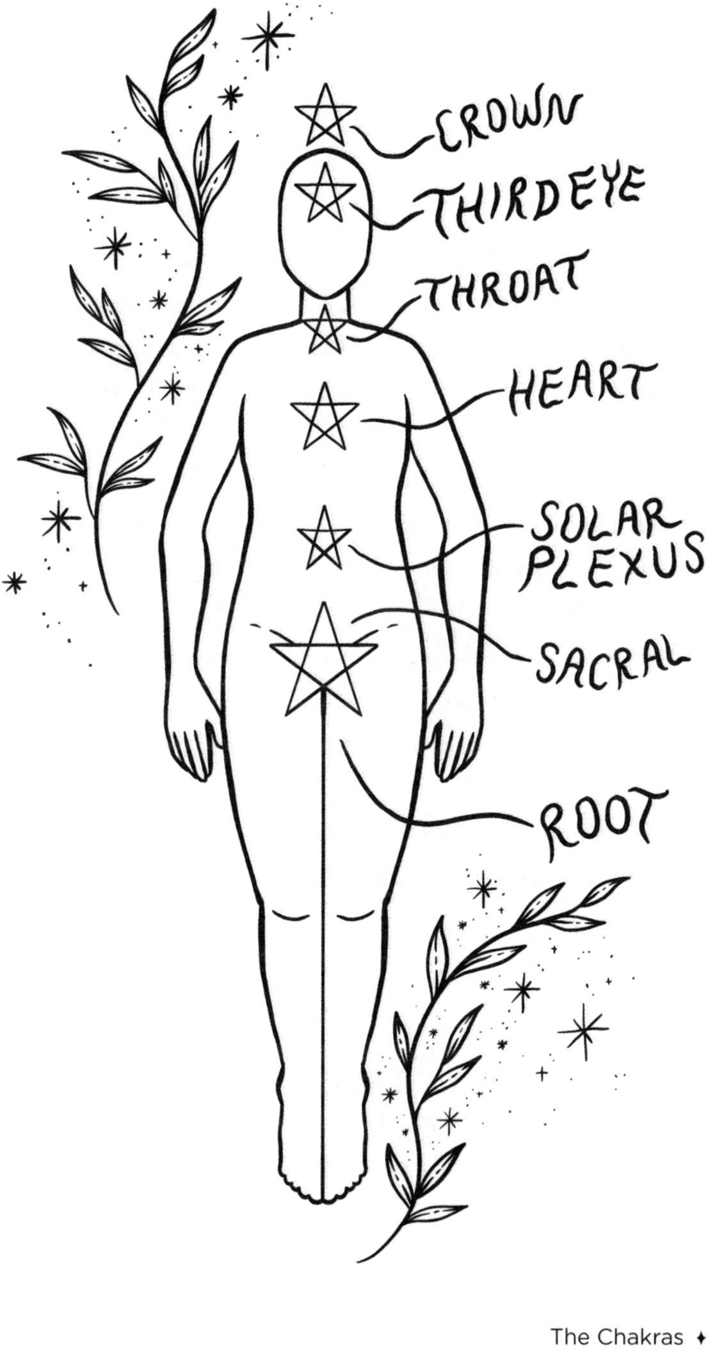
CROWN
THIRDEYE
THROAT
HEART
SOLAR
PLEXUS
SACRAL
ROOT

Root Chakra (Red)

SANSKRIT NAME: Muladhara (root support)

ELEMENT: Earth

KEYWORD: Home

The Root chakra is the first chakra, located at the base of the spine. It is home to our sense of security, survival, and stability. Like the roots of a tree, the Root chakra is the foundation for the energetic system. It is also the root of our collective consciousness, and the chakra by which we connect to others on an earthly level.

When balanced, the Root chakra allows us to feel grounded, stable, and still. We feel comfortable and supported. When unbalanced, we might feel anxious, antsy, unwelcome, alone, stressed, or out of place.

Correspondences: the color red, root vegetables, Waning Moon and Dark Moon, red calcite, hematite, black obsidian, red jasper, smoky quartz, black tourmaline, bloodstone, ruby, garnet, pressing one's feet into the earth, heavy blankets, wintertime, Capricorn, Taurus

Sacral Chakra (Orange)

SANSKRIT NAME: Svadisthana (sweetness)

ELEMENT: Water

KEYWORD: Passion

The second chakra is the Sacral, located in the lower abdomen and the sacral area of the spine. It also influences the pelvic area. The Sacral chakra rules over sexuality, intimacy, passion, pleasure, emotions, and creation (so, while the Throat chakra rules over creativity, the Sacral chakra is also a big influence in this area, especially if the creativity being conjured is more passion, feral, and in the body).

When the Sacral chakra is balanced and open, we are more likely to feel a flow of passion, joy, play, and excitement. For some, this might manifest as a higher sex drive, while for others it might manifest as an energetic drive to pursue passions and desires. Balanced, this chakra is a point of joy and pleasure, in all forms. When unbalanced, we might feel frustrated or stuck, and there may be negative thoughts directed at ourselves.

Correspondences: the color orange, abstract art, Full Moon, sex toys, carnelian, amber, orange calcite, tiger's eye, bumblebee jasper, cuprite, red jade, sunstone, satin, swimming, summertime, orange roses, Scorpio, Leo

Solar Plexus (Yellow)

SANSKRIT NAME: Manipura (lustrous gem)

ELEMENT: Fire

KEYWORD: Confidence

The Solar Plexus is the third chakra, located in the solar plexus (just above the belly button), ruling over will, empowerment, assertiveness, and sense of self. It translates emotion into terms we can understand and facilitates transformation.

When balanced, the Solar Plexus chakra allows us to see things through to completion, approach situations with a level head, and think clearly about what's going on in our lives. It helps us manage expectations and goals, while giving us the space to navigate what needs to get done, and in what order. We feel like our best selves, energized and confident. When the Solar Plexus chakra is unbalanced or blocked, we might find ourselves fixating, micromanaging, and getting stressed about minor details. It can be difficult to trust ourselves or let go of what needs to be released. We might not feel like ourselves.

Correspondences: the color yellow, lists, organization, citrine, golden healer quartz, mookaite, yellow jade, golden beryl (heliodor), yellow jasper, golden calcite, summertime, raw silk, an outfit that makes you feel confident, dandelions, sunflowers, Virgo, Aries

Heart Chakra (Green/Pink)

SANSKRIT NAME: Anahata (unstruck)

ELEMENT: Air

KEYWORD: Love

The Heart chakra is the fourth chakra, located in the center of your chest. It is the central point of the whole system, uniting the chakras in the upper part of your body (the Throat, Third Eye, and Crown; the more spiritual chakras) with those in the lower part (the Solar Plexus, Sacral, and the Root; the more earthly and animal chakras). The Heart chakra oversees all forms of love, from romantic love to platonic love to compassion of self.

When it is balanced, the Heart chakra connects us to feelings of wholeness and pure universal love, giving us the space to love ourselves and others. We feel compassion for others and ourselves, and we have the space to let love rule over more of our decisions and conscious efforts. When the Heart chakra is unbalanced or blocked, we may find ourselves feeling self-loathing, bitterness, and a lack of empathy and compassion toward others (as well as ourselves).

Correspondences: the colors green and pink, springtime, gifts from loved ones, Valentine's Day, Venus, pastels, rose quartz, rhodochrosite, chrysoprase, pink tourmaline, emerald, smoky rose quartz, pink danburite, rhodonite, green sapphire, chrysocolla, Libra, Cancer

Throat Chakra (Blue)

SANSKRIT NAME: Visudda (purification)

ELEMENT: Sound

KEYWORD: Expression

The fifth chakra, the Throat, is located (as you may have guessed) in the throat. It is connected to all forms of communication and expression, especially through sound. The Throat chakra is connected to all forms of creativity, but especially those that are acts of self-expression, use sound, or allow a flow of ideas to be communicated to others.

When balanced, the Throat chakra helps us find connection with the world and with others, aiding in our ability to clearly communicate thoughts, ideas, and emotions to others, as well as with ourselves. When the Throat chakra is unbalanced or blocked, it can be difficult to communicate or to express oneself.

Correspondences: the color blue, Mercury, cell phones, letters, spoken language, singing, sound bowls, sound baths, songbirds, blue quartz, blue calcite, angelite, kyanite, lazulite, blue lace agate, sodalite, slippery elm, oil of oregano, blue silk, New Moon, Sagittarius, Gemini

Third Eye Chakra (Indigo)

SANSKRIT NAME: Ajna (to perceive, to command)

ELEMENT: Light

KEYWORD: Awareness

Also called the Forehead or Brow chakra, the sixth chakra is located in the middle of your forehead, just above your eyebrows. It is connected to psychic gifts, intuition, imagination, and the ability to see (both physical and divine worlds).

When balanced, the Third Eye chakra allows us to be more aware, in a physical sense of self, and in a greater sense that connects us to the universe and Spirit. When it's balanced, our sense of intuition is stronger, and it's easier to access psychic abilities. When the Third Eye chakra is unbalanced, there is a distinct lack of self-awareness, causing us to not be fully aware of ourselves or the space we occupy. We may have trouble seeing the truth or trusting our intuition. You can still access and utilize your intuition and psychic gifts if the Third Eye chakra is blocked, but the way you share the information may come across as tone-deaf or ignorant. You may also be weak to psychic attacks.

Correspondences: the color indigo, light, outer space, the all-seeing eye, the Moon, Neptune, azurite, Mount Shasta opal, blue halite, iolite, lapis lazuli, afghanite, blue obsidian, amethyst, Pisces, Aquarius

Crown Chakra (Violet/White)

SANSKRIT NAME: Sahashara (thousandfold)

ELEMENT: Thought

KEYWORD: Clarity

The seventh chakra is the Crown, located on the top of the head. This chakra connects us to the divine, the universal, wisdom, and our highest selves. The Crown chakra rules over understanding and knowing. It is openness, all knowledge, Akashic records, and the source of ultimate liberation and manifestation. The Crown chakra is all, and our connection to absolutely everything. It is connected to spirituality and enlightenment.

When balanced and open, the Crown chakra allows us to access divine information, and introduces us to ourselves and who we truly are. We think clearly, and can access and interpret our thoughts easily. When the Crown chakra is blocked or unbalanced, we may feel uncoordinated, confused, or uncertain. There may also be a lack of focus and a discomfort with one's sense of self.

Correspondences: the colors violet and white, amethyst, all planets, lilac kunzite, aurora quartz, cathedral quartz, apophyllite, diamond, phenacite, white jade, all signs

Along with using a pendulum to determine whether there are any blockages or imbalances, you can opt to work with a specific chakra and what it represents by using a pendulum made out of a corresponding crystal.

Chapter 14

CLEARING OR CLEANSING A PENDULUM

You've used your pendulum to clear something else, like a crystal or an aura. You've been using it for some time. Is it time to cleanse it? Is it time to clear its energy? Is it even necessary to do so?

In general, I don't think it's totally necessary to clear or cleanse magical tools as much as people seem to suggest. It's one thing if you're working with clients or doing work for another person. In those cases, you will want to clear and cleanse after every client or friend to remove their energy from the tool. But for many of us magical practitioners, the goal is not to involve other people. I do a lot of work for clients, but that's because it's part of my personal path. There are still massive swaths of my practice that I don't let others see. I have tarot decks that are just for me. I have secrets of my craft that I will never share. I don't post photos of my altar spaces on the internet. The contents of my grimoire will likely never be seen by more than a handful of people.

My relationship with my pendulum is actually very personal. The work I do with it is largely just for me, and I don't think I'll ever do pendulum work for clients. So, while I do have tools that need to be cleared and cleansed after I do work for others, there are some tools in my arsenal (pendulum included) that don't interact with others' energy. I might cleanse them occasionally, but it's exceedingly rare.

If you're the only one interacting with a magical tool, it's really up to you as to how often you clear it or cleanse it. I used to clear my tarot decks often, but I fell out of the habit because I find that the more I use a deck, the better readings I get for myself. Sometimes it is beneficial to have your energetic fingerprints all over the tools you use. It's a sign of familiarity, comfort, and intimacy. You might never feel the need to cleanse your tools. You might choose to do it every day. Either option is completely fine, because it is a personal choice based on your comfort and individual needs.

Let's say that you do wish to clear your pendulum. You have several ways of doing that:

* Use another pendulum to clear the pendulum, as you would a crystal.
* Place the pendulum in the light of the Full Moon.
* Place the pendulum on top of a piece of selenite or in a selenite bowl.
* Let the pendulum cleanse itself by allowing it to swing in a circle until it winds down to a stationary position.
* Visualize white light purifying the pendulum.
* Run the pendulum under cool water (before doing this, make sure that the pendulum isn't made of anything that might conflict with water, especially if it's a crystal pendulum). Dry it well to make sure any metal bits don't rust.
* Pass the pendulum through incense smoke.
* Call upon your guides and Spirits to remove any unwanted/unneeded/uninvited energies from the pendulum.

Once your pendulum is cleared, you don't have to wait to use it again, but it is entirely up to the individual and what makes sense for them, and their magical practice. For instance, if I'm clearing tools that I use for client readings or work, I will do something quick in between sessions, but then I'll do thorough and intensive clearings when I'm not planning on doing any work for a bit. Clearing can be done on a need-by-need, case-by-case, basis.

Cleansing a pendulum is a bit more intense, and more involved. Think of it as completely erasing the pendulum. You'll likely need to recalibrate the pendulum when you're finished cleansing it. Cleansing can be useful if you received a pendulum secondhand, or if you are choosing to let go of a pendulum you've been using. For cleansing a pendulum, I recommend taking a few days during a Full Moon or Dark Moon phase, combining several of the techniques used for clearing. Start by physically cleaning it with a soft cloth, and then choose the cleansing options that speak to you. Take your time with the process, and continue until the pendulum feels truly neutral.

Conclusion

PENDULUM MAGIC AND THE EXPANSE OF CHOICE

When I started experimenting with pendulums, I didn't know where to start. I struggled with a lot of the resources, and it was certainly an example of something that seemed *too simple*. When something feels too easy or too simple, I tend to feel like I'm somehow cheating by doing it. Surely, if it's that easy, it's not going to work. Surely, if it's that easy, I'm missing something. I have to regularly remind myself that just because something feels easy doesn't mean that it's not right. It doesn't mean that it's going to be ineffective. I recently started painting again, and just let myself enjoy it. The process came naturally, and it felt easy. Something being easy just means that it's coming naturally, or that it's meant to be straightforward and user friendly. Painting feels easy because I'm good at it, and I enjoy it. Pendulum divination is easy because it's a form of divination that *is* easy, and it's meant to be easy.

I can't be the only witch or magical practitioner who doubts and questions my abilities when it feels easy. I can't be the only one who feels weary of answers when they come through without struggle. Magic doesn't have to be a struggle. Magic is wonderful because it can be easy, and to the point. Magic can be straightforward. If the magic is effective, you don't have to focus too heavily on why it's effective. If you bake a cake, you probably don't sit there wondering how heat was able to transform a raw ingredient into something edible and delicious. You can trust the process because it is what it is. You can trust magic because it works. If the cake is still raw in the middle, you pop it back in the oven and try again. You don't dismiss the whole thing because it didn't quite work on the first try. Sometimes small adjustments need to be made, but that doesn't mean that the whole process needs to be dismissed or thrown away.

Pendulums are straightforward. Using a pendulum is a method of divination that is simple, and maybe that's part of the reason it's easy to believe that ancient people may have used pendulums as divination tools. We don't need to overthink the process, or how it's done. Sure, there are physics at work, and calculations can be done around the swing of a pendulum, but you don't have to know all of that to appreciate the pendulum as a magical tool and to use it in your day-to-day life. There is a finite number of ways a pendulum can move, but an infinite number of ways to interact with it and understand. A pendulum isn't like flipping a coin (a form of divination in its own right). At first glance, it will seem like a pendulum is only capable of yes or no, but as we learned in this book, there are so many more ways to interact with this deceptively simple tool.

I'm nonbinary, leaning transmasc, with a lot of gender fluidity in how I present myself to the world. My gender identity is part of the lens in which I see the world. While researching the pendulum and thinking about its possibilities, I found myself thinking about gender. Gender, just like the pendulum, represents more than two possibilities. We live in a very binary world, and it is reflected in every aspect of modern life. Yet, many cultures have more than two genders. A lot of cultures don't look at everything in such harsh black-and-white terms. Most of the ideas and understanding we have around gender, bodies, and identity are cemented into our existence through the structures of capitalism, colonization, and white supremacy.

A lot of magical schools of thought uphold these ideas of the binary. Black magic versus white magic. Good versus evil. Male versus female. It all boils down to one versus the other, even though there is so much room for fluidity, overlap, or total removal of a binary in general.

Back in 2021, I made a digital zine about the dangers of binary thinking. The main criticism I received was that certain neurodivergences can make it difficult to not think in binaries. Sure, I get that. But my point was (and is) that binary thinking goes deeper than problem solving and day-to-day social interactions. Even the idea that being neurodivergent means that certain things are challenges or impossibilities for all neurodivergent people is binary thinking, and it's harmful. It's ableist to put limitations on other people based on what we think they're capable of. It's harmful to limit ourselves based on what other people have told us. All or nothing isn't a way to live.

Binary thinking (also known as dichotomous thinking) is when complex concepts, ideas, and problems are simplified into being one side or another. This means looking at things as stark opposites. Our brains tend to be dichotomizing machines, simplifying the world into true/false, good/bad, or is/is not. Thinking in binaries generally prevents us from being accurate in our perceptions, because we're ignoring the nuances that exist in all situations. I constantly find myself creating binary narratives in my thinking. When this happens, I know to step back and look at the arguments I'm making. I think everything needs some level of gray just to help keep things interesting. Culture, brain structure, politics, upbringing, religion, whatever—they are often treated as one or the other, all or nothing, and so forth. But integration and expansion between worlds can make for some radical newness. What else is possible?

Contrary to popular belief, there are always more than two choices. In Western society, especially under capitalism, we are generally forced into boxes, and demands are made that we must define, choose, label. Cis-heteronormative patriarchal society wants us to comply with arbitrary rules, rules that stem from white supremacy and colonization. We are taught to believe that we will be punished if we ask to see behind the proverbial third door. Gender, and pendulums, can teach us the benefit of not only acknowledging that third door, but opening it and exploring.

Pendulums are often presented as swinging one way for "yes," another way for "no." Any time it is taught that pendulums have two functions, and can only carry dichotomous information, it upholds the notion that there are only ever two options. One or two. Chocolate or vanilla. Black or white. Door one or door two.

What else is there? What exists behind door number 3? Looking for possibilities, beyond the known and accepted and understood, is *exciting.* There are always an infinite number of possibilities and ideas and thought forms once we step outside of what is already established. Think about the Oscar-winning film *Everything Everywhere All at Once.* The concept of infinity and endless choice and having power over our choices can be . . . a bit overwhelming. But it's also oddly liberating. We are in control of our decisions, including our decision to recognize that there are more than two choices, and there's more than what we see with our eyes. And if we made the wrong choice? We'll never know, so it doesn't matter.

Suddenly, the pendulum swings in a circle. Clockwise, counterclockwise. It goes still, vibrating in place. Does its subtle turning in place carry a message? You get out a half-circle pendulum board with the slices, each offering an option. You go deeper, but by using a talking board. Suddenly, it can communicate entire stories and ideas. The expanse of choice even leaves the realm of the question and answer completely, shifting into the potential for healing and spell-casting. The pendulum is not a dichotomous entity, and neither are we as people.

Pendulums can offer a lot of direction and guidance in terms of just how many options and choices lay before us at any time. Yes, you can ask a simple "yes" or "no" question, but you can also consider all of the information and possibilities. There are countless directions. Nothing is linear, and nothing is black and white. All of life is a spectrum of grays and a spectrum of colors. You can demand more information, more answers, because it is available to you. You don't have to comply to "this or that." There is an expanse of direction, options, decisions, and choices. You just have to ask.

The pendulum can teach us lessons about what it means to be human, and what it means to change. Not everything needs to be rigid or set in stone. We don't need to divide everything into binaries, and that extends beyond identity. Binary systems are meant for computers, not us. The pendulum is a unique magical object and divination tool because it is so simple, but it offers its own unique type of complexity. The pendulum is not only an invitation to seek answers, but also to connect with yourself.

RESOURCES

FURTHER READING

New World Witchery: A Trove of North American Folk Magic by Cory Thomas Hutcheson

Parable of the Sower by Octavia E. Butler

Playful Magic by Janina Renee

BIBLIOGRAPHY

A Witches' Bible: The Complete Witches' Handbook by Janet and Stewart Farrar

Curious Myths of the Middle Ages by Sabine Baring-Gould

The Encyclopedia of Crystals by Judy Hall

Gemstones and Color (and a Whole Lot More) by Marie Williams Cornelio, channeled through Marjorie Buckley Turcotte

The Kybalion by William Walker Atkinson

Mastering the Tarot by Eden Gray

The Nature of the Physical World by Arthur Eddington

The New Tarot Handbook by Rachel Pollack

The Occult Sciences: A Compendium of Transcendental Doctrine and Experiment by Arthur Edward Waite

Pendulum Magic for Beginners by Richard Webster

The Roman History of Ammianus Marcellinus

Solitary Witch: The Ultimate Book of Shadows for the New Generation by Silver RavenWolf

ACKNOWLEDGMENTS

This book was written primarily on a vintage Olympia typewriter in my home in New Brunswick, Canada, on the unceded territory of the Wabanaki, Wolastoqiyik, and Mi'kma'ki First Nations. I'm grateful to have my home on this land, and have it be the place where I make magic, write, and create.

Many thanks to: my spouse Sarah for your constant and endless support; my mom, my dad in Spirit, and my siblings Jake and Katharine; Octavia E. Butler for being a guiding spirit; my editor Kate; my friends Ash, Kaitlin, and Reed; Chase for your thoughts on ceramic pendulums; my four cats; and anyone else who helped me or gave me valuable insight during the research and writing processes. I appreciate all of you endlessly. I'm not going to say that I couldn't do this without you, but it would be a lot harder if you weren't present in my life.

INDEX

D

E

F

Q

R

S

ABOUT THE AUTHOR

FOX TAYLOR (A.K.A. THE WITCH CRUCIFIXVI) is a nonbinary artist and writer, currently residing in New Brunswick, Canada, with their spouse and four cats. They are a neurodivergent weirdo who enjoys textile art, making comics, watching movies, and playing video games. They are an Aries, and it shows. Their first book, *Sigil Craft*, was published by Union Square in 2023.

Contrary to popular belief, they are not an actual fox.

PENDULUM BOARDS

Ready to start using a pendulum to answer your questions? The following selection of pendulum boards will help you begin your journey. Included are ten half-circle pendulum boards to help you answer your magical questions, three blank boards to fill in based on your own individual needs and queries, and two circular boards, one with the English alphabet and one for yes/no/maybe questions. These pendulum boards will offer a good starting point for readings while you practice and further hone your craft.

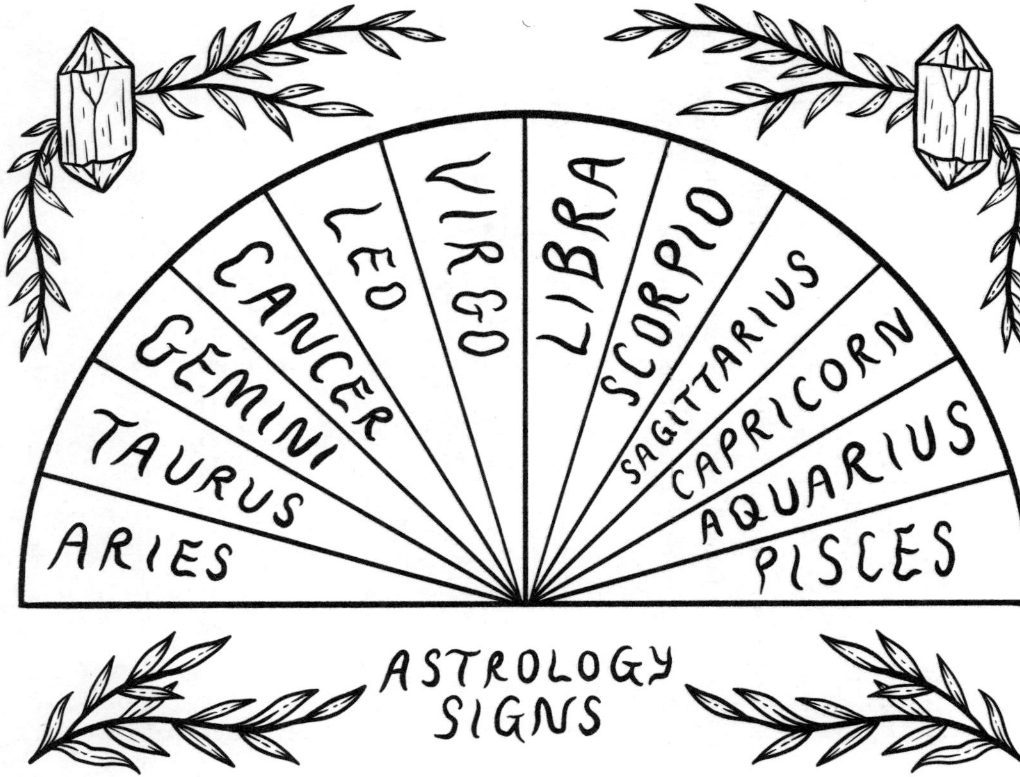
ARIES
TAURUS
GEMINI
CANCER
LEO
VIRGO
LIBRA
SCORPIO
SAGITTARIUS
CAPRICORN
AQUARIUS
PISCES
ASTROLOGY
SIGNS

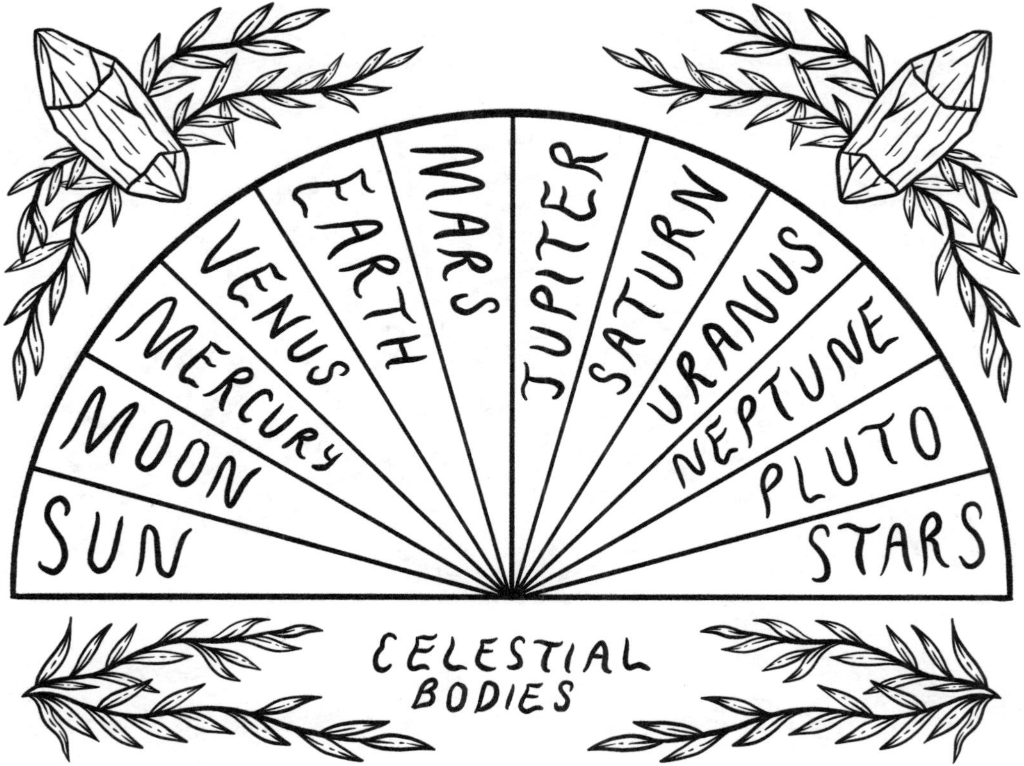
SUN
MOON
MERCURY
VENUS
EARTH
MARS
JUPITER
SATURN
URANUS
NEPTUNE
PLUTO
STARS
CELESTIAL BODIES

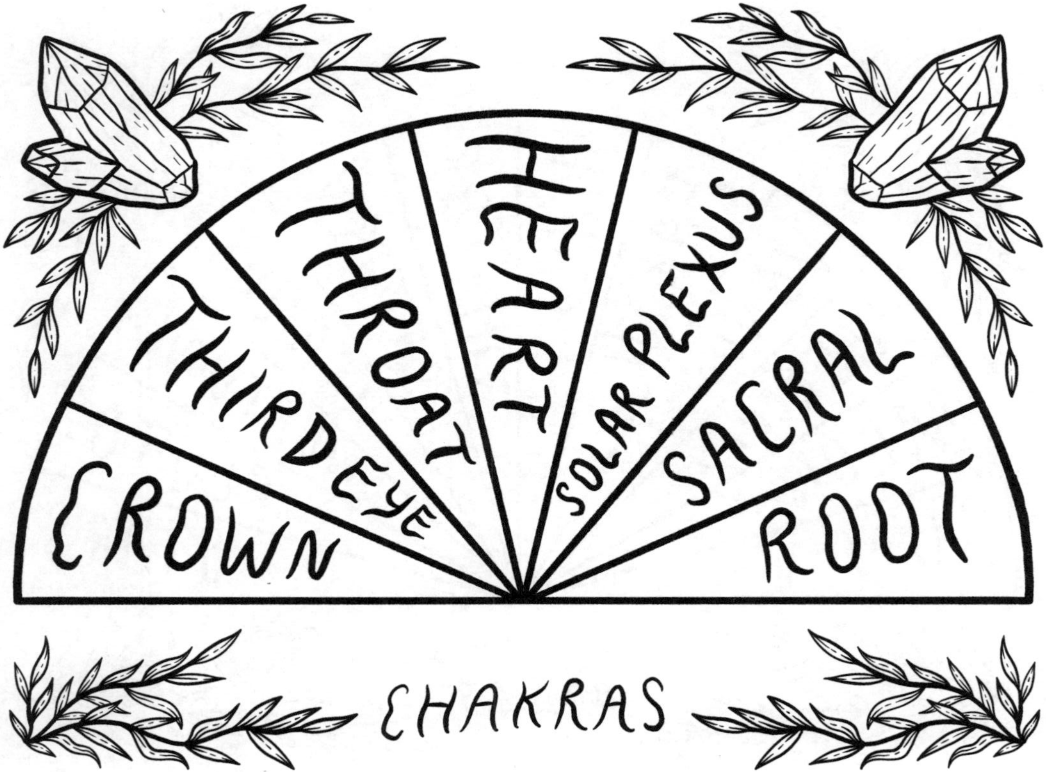
CROWN
THIRD EYE
THROAT
HEART
SOLAR PLEXUS
SACRAL
ROOT
CHAKRAS

BLACK
WHITE
RED
ORANGE
YELLOW
GREEN
BLUE
PURPLE
MULTICOLOR
GRAY
BROWN
PINK
COLORS

ZERO
ONE
TWO
THREE
FOUR
FIVE
SIX
SEVEN
EIGHT
NINE
TEN
HIGHER
NUMBERS

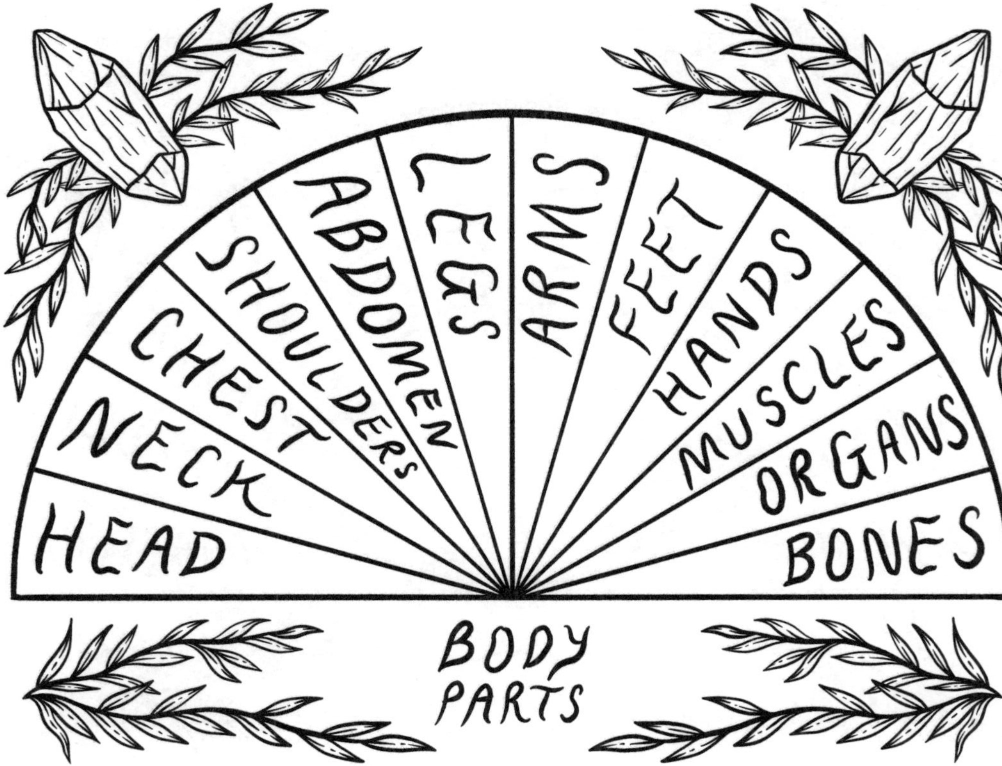
HEAD
NECK
CHEST
SHOULDERS
ABDOMEN
LEGS
ARMS
FEET
HANDS
MUSCLES
ORGANS
BONES
BODY PARTS

CRYSTALS
QUARTZ
BLACK TOURMALINE
ROSE QUARTZ
CARNELIAN
AMETHYST
JASPER
ONYX
CALCITE
SELENITE
PYRITE
LAPIS LAZULI
KYANITE

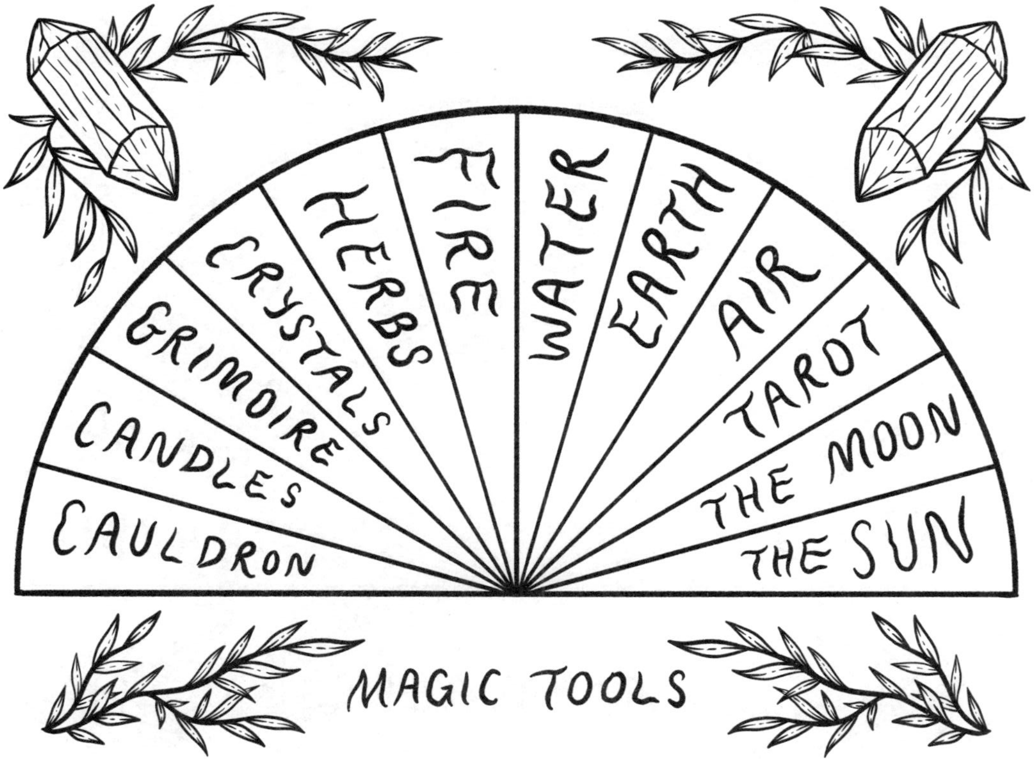
CAULDRON
CANDLES
GRIMOIRE
CRYSTALS
HERBS
FIRE
WATER
EARTH
AIR
TAROT
THE MOON
THE SUN
MAGIC TOOLS

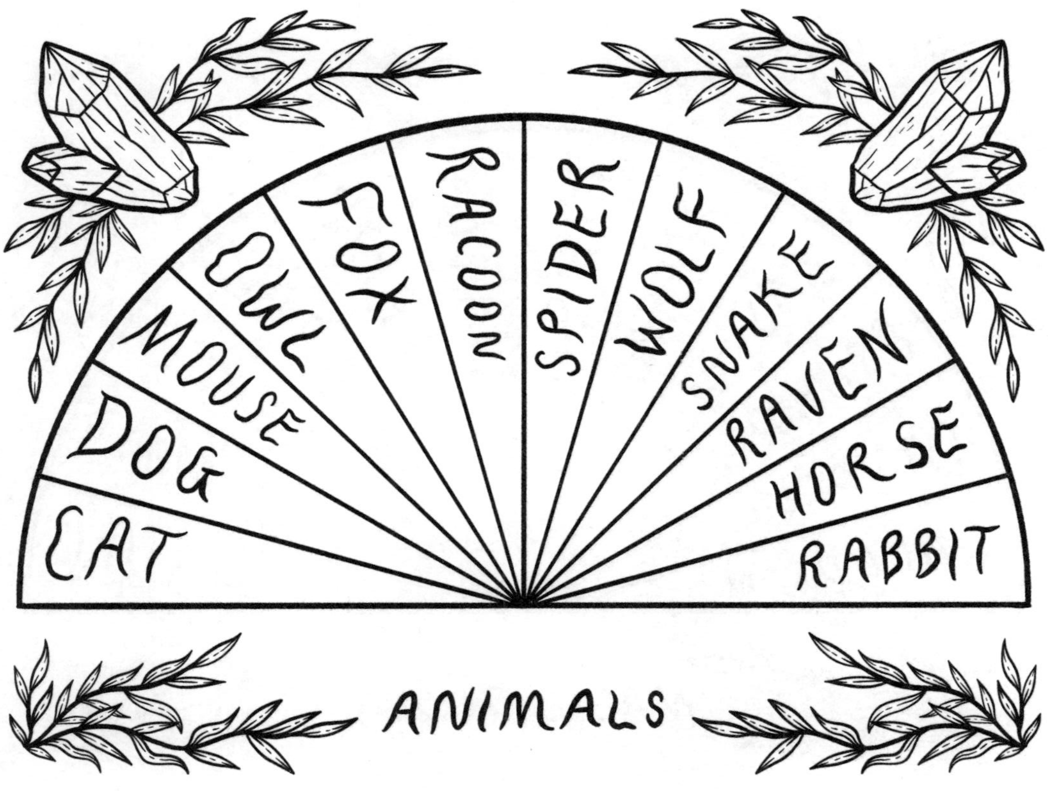
CAT
DOG
MOUSE
OWL
FOX
RACOON
SPIDER
WOLF
SNAKE
RAVEN
HORSE
RABBIT
ANIMALS

COVEN
ANCESTRAL
CRYSTAL
CELESTIAL
GREEN
HEDGE
BANEFUL
FOLK
KITCHEN
HOUSE
CEREMONIAL
CHAOS
SCHOOLS OF MAGIC

COPY AND
FILL IN

COPY AND
FILL IN

COPY AND
FILL IN

A B C D E F G H I J K L M N O P Q R S T U V W X Y Z

NO
MAYBE
REPHRASE
YES
YES
REPHRASE
MAYBE
NO